DESOLATION AND DECAY OF MAINE

THE RICH TRUTHS ABOUT MAINE'S EERIE PAST

CRYSTAL EASTMAN

AMERICA THROUGH TIME

This book is dedicated to the love of my life, Dale Peaslee Jr., for always embracing adventure with me. Convincing someone to embark on multiple trips to explore abandoned properties in Maine is no small feat. Your unwavering support and companionship mean the world to me. The memories we have created together hold a special place in my heart. Thank you for being my partner in this journey and in this life.

America Through Time®
An imprint of Sutton Publishing Inc.
www.through-time.com

First published 2025
Reprinted 2026

ISBN 978-1-63499-546-7

Typeset in Trade Gothic 10pt on 15pt
Printed and bound in the United States of America

PREFACE

As people age, we develop interests and hobbies that we are passionate about. However, pursuing these interests of ours can sometimes be more challenging than anticipated. Time often appears to be a hindrance, or perhaps we are simply moving too quickly in our own lives. Fortunately, I discovered a hobby that allows me to pause, reflect, and appreciate the beauty of life.

From the time I was just a young girl, I found a fascination with photography as I picked up my mother's camera. As I matured, I realized the preciousness of time and how capturing the world through my lens could immortalize moments that would otherwise slip away. I found joy in capturing moments that brought a smile to someone's face or things that caught my eye. Taking a photography class in high school was a pivotal moment for me. I had the unique opportunity to develop film in a darkroom, an experience that remains vivid in my memory even to this day.

Photography evolved from a mere interest into a deep passion for me. Initially, my focus was on capturing family portraits after purchasing a camera in 2014. However, years later, I made a shift and decided to stop photographing people, choosing instead to venture across Maine in search of captivating locations. My interests led me to explore abandoned places, driven by a newfound sense of curiosity and adventure that emerged during the COVID-19 pandemic.

Prior to this, a lasting impression was left on me in 2013 after riding down a dirt road, through a haunted ghost town in New Hampshire. As my friends and I were casually driving along the road, a young bull moose unexpectedly collided with my side of the back-passenger door. It then continued to trot down the road to its mother. The encounter was both astonishing and alarming.

In the spring of 2016, I visited the Tip-A-Canoe campground in Porter, Maine. The dilapidated fields, overgrown tennis courts, and eerie remains of an old pool filled with debris painted a haunting yet intriguing picture. Venturing inside, I felt a sense of both excitement and apprehension, unsure of what I might encounter next. These experiences and encounters along the way primed me to have an open mind.

From capturing the nostalgia of my grandfather's old cars to exploring the forgotten history of places like Tip-A-Canoe, each encounter added a new layer to my developing path as a photographer and explorer. The challenges and uncertainties of 2020 only served to deepen my resolve to continue exploring and documenting the undiscovered treasures that lie in the pine tree state.

Delving into the history and narratives of these structures sparks my inquisitiveness. I ponder about the lives that once thrived before me and the reasons that led to their abandonment. Did financial struggles force families to leave their homes behind? Did time simply take its toll on these once vibrant spaces? The mystery and intrigue surrounding these places fuels my passion for photography, driving me to uncover its history before it's long forgotten.

CONTENTS

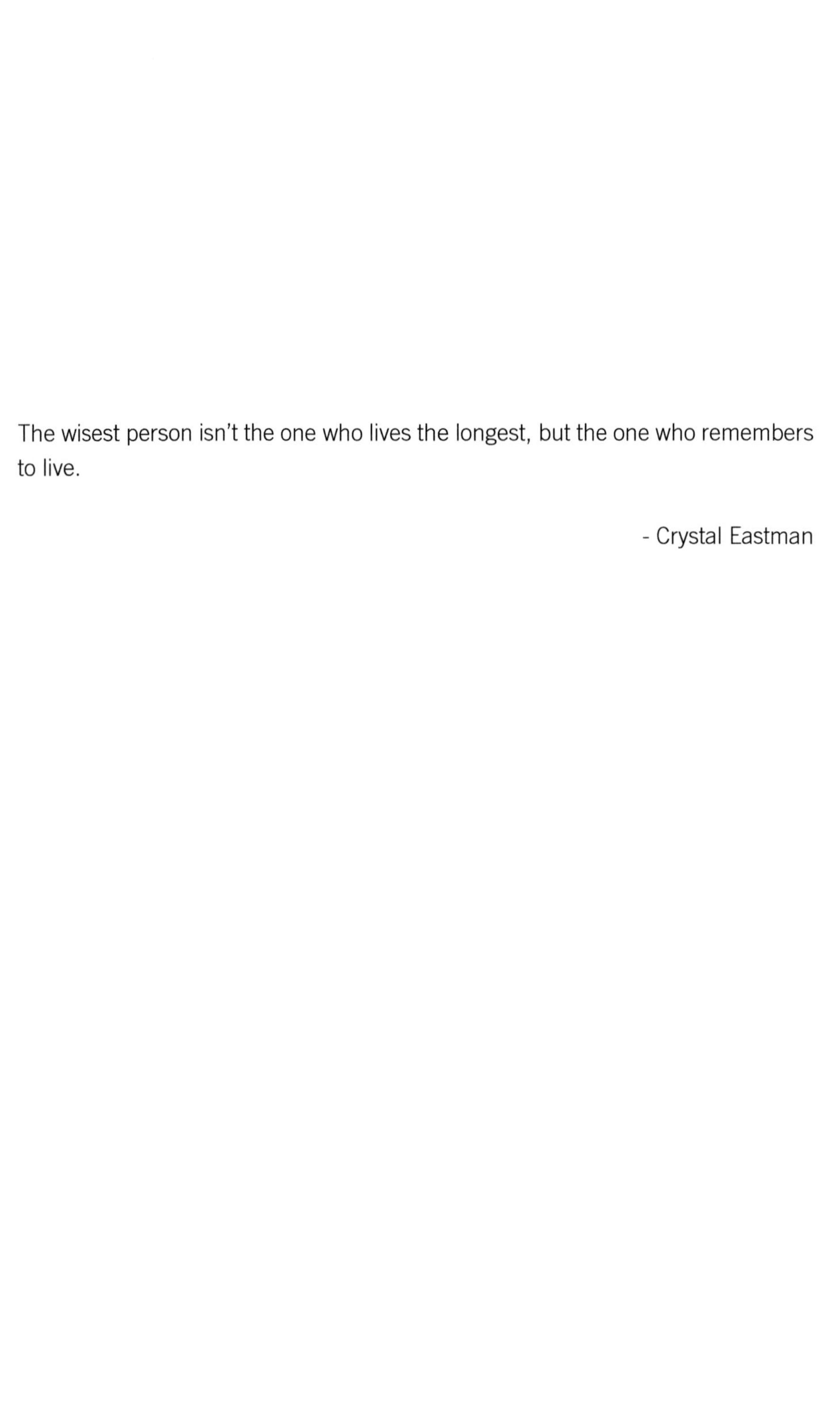

The wisest person isn't the one who lives the longest, but the one who remembers to live.

- Crystal Eastman

INTRODUCTION

Maine is truly a magnificent state. From its vast ocean to potato fields, the diversity of Maine's landscapes is astounding. A round trip from the bottom to the top takes about twelve hours total. It's difficult to comprehend the sheer size of Maine until you witness it firsthand. Discovering abandoned buildings can be akin to finding a needle in a haystack, but at times, they stand out prominently against the backdrop of the state's beauty.

They have long been a magnet for urban explorers and adventurers seeking to uncover hidden treasures and secrets. Exploring these empty spaces can be a thrilling and sometimes dangerous experience, as explorers navigate through crumbling floors, peeling paint, and decaying structures. The sense of mystery and discovery that comes with exploring abandoned buildings adds to their appeal. These buildings are often remnants of a bygone era, with architectural features and design elements that reflect the trends and styles of the past. They tend to serve as time capsules, offering a glimpse into the history and culture of a specific time period. For example, abandoned factories may reveal the industrial heritage of a city, while abandoned mansions may speak to the opulence of a previous era.

As these neglected architectural gems teeter on the brink of decay and potential demolition, they embody a poignant loss of our cultural heritage. The disregard and absence of preservation endeavors put at stake the intricate narratives and historical significance that these places carry, ultimately eroding our shared identity and ties to the past.

Through a concerted effort to acknowledge the value of select structures and implement proactive preservation measures, we can ensure the protection of these irreplaceable landmarks for the enjoyment and enlightenment of future generations.

Regrettably, not every location is fortunate enough to be saved from destruction. Currently, my aspiration is to capture the essence of these enticing sites through my photography, aiming to share their enduring legacy with a broader audience. This endeavor seeks to serve as a valuable record of these architectural treasures.

Join me on an exploration of the haunting realm of abandoned buildings, where every cracked window and crumbling brick murmurs a story from a previous time. I will also explore a chapter detailing my first paranormal investigation, which occurred inside an old nursing home. Together, we shall investigate the beauty, enigma, and odd allure of these forsaken spaces, unearthing the concealed treasures that reside within their confines.

1

THE HOUSE OF A SOLDIER'S DESCENDANT

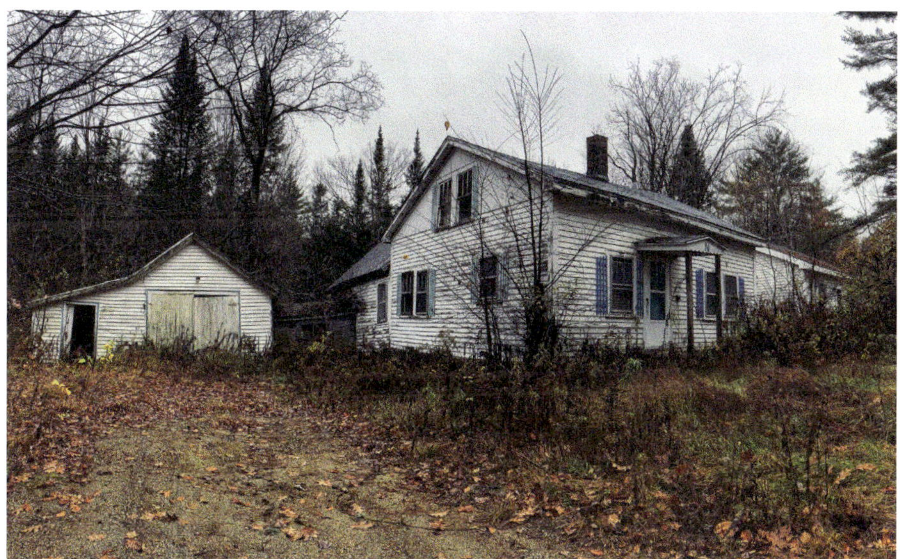

Each time I went by this house I always wondered what treasures were inside. I'm glad I convinced myself to go in. You can learn a lot about history and people from the layout of someone's house, deserted in the middle of the woods.

Every time I drove by this old house nestled in the tall grass, I gazed out the window. It always caught my attention, so I finally convinced myself to stop. A deep breath filled my lungs as I felt the urge to explore its mysterious interior. I quietly exhaled, while also wanting to be respectful as this was not my house. The look of it hinted at years of neglect. With no signs prohibiting entry, I walked through not only one, but four open doorways, where there had once been doors, only to be astounded by what lay before me.

Walking in, the evocative atmosphere enveloped me. It was as if it were twenty years ago and Grandma was about to enter the kitchen in her apron to pull a pie out of the oven. That familiar feeling still lingered. A journal revealed that this was the home to a great, great, great granddaughter of one of the founding fathers of Sumner, Maine. This harked back to a time when it was still part of Massachusetts and known as Butterfield Plantation. The land where her family had grown up had been awarded to her great (x3) grandfather for his service in the Revolutionary War. At the time of the town's establishment in 1798, the war had already been over for fifteen years. She had decided to settle in East Sumner, not too far away—a trend I noticed my parents adopted, both only living short distances from their parents as well. It wasn't until my generation came to fruition that I branched out to live further North.

Diving deeper into the past, I stumbled upon a journal from 1868 that showed insight into the challenges of medical care in those times. The entries showed me the hardships faced by the family, with limited access to medicine and reliance on home remedies. The house itself seemed to tell its own story, filled with personal items like a sewing machine and a piano that I'm sure would light up the room. It exuded the essence of a cultured woman who once lived here, with traces of her belongings such as a typewritten poem and hand sewn dolls. Wandering through the house, I discovered bouts of entertainment from a simpler time. From paper dolls to vintage records, and home movie reels, back when such things held one's attention.

The presence of a metal lunchbox and a wooden bread box made me smile. A handwritten letter from 1867, penned with a quill, stood out in a cash box. The sight of that and a corded wall phone brought back memories of a time when communication was slower and more deliberate. For a few seconds I tried picturing myself living back then, when life's pace seemed much calmer.

Presents still wrapped were scattered about near a small Christmas tree, adorned with a name tag on each of them that read, "Just for display." Among the family treasures left behind was a vinyl record of *Shirley Temple* lying casually mixed in with a pile of others on the floor. I picked it up to have a closer look, setting it on the counter. Memories flooded back from being at my grandparents' house as a child, watching *Shirley Temple* ads come on TV. One couldn't miss her voice and those curly locks, that's for sure.

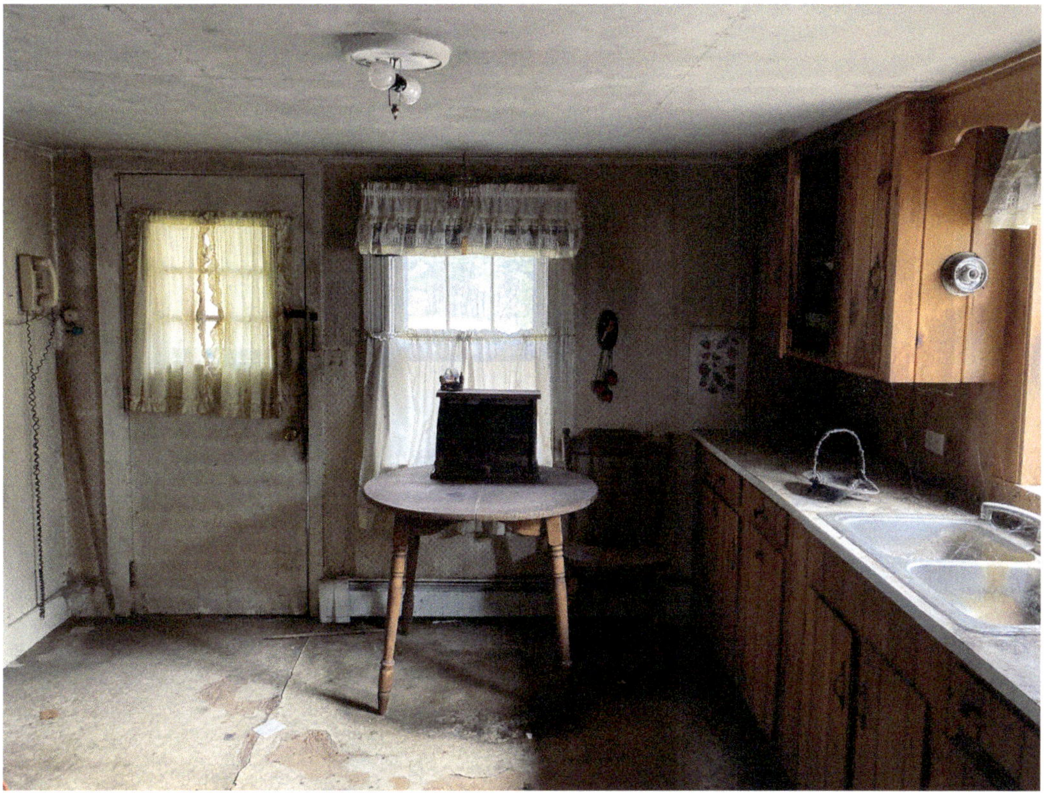

This kitchen was very inviting, now home to multiple spiders.

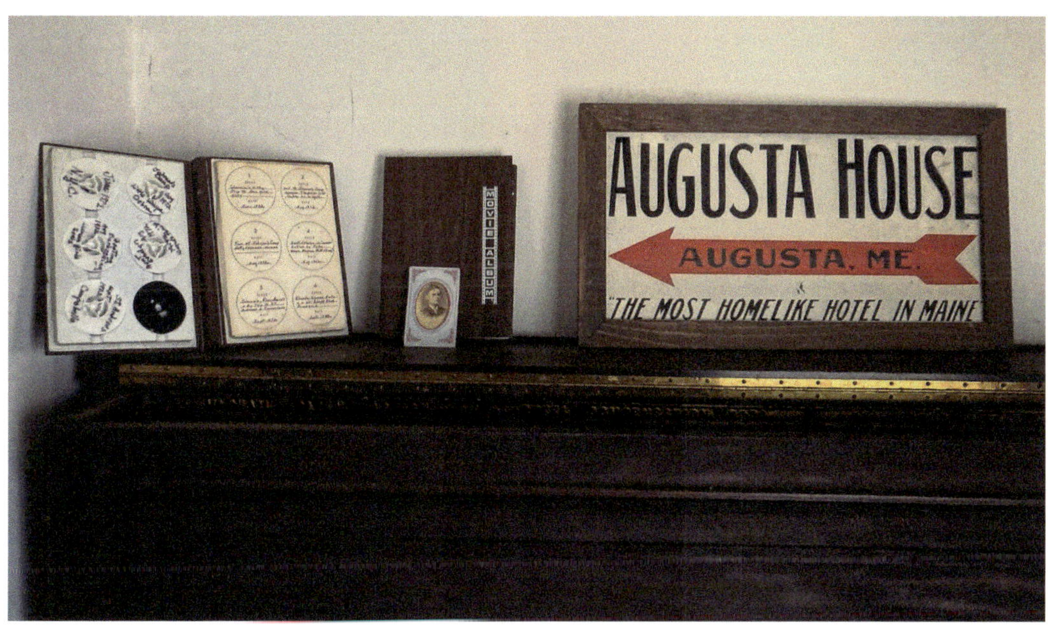

Home movie reels reminded me of a time when life moved at a slower pace. The wooden sign from the old hotel intrigued me to look up its history, teaching me even more about our state. Investigating further, I confirmed my importance in documenting such structures as I discovered the building had been demolished years ago.

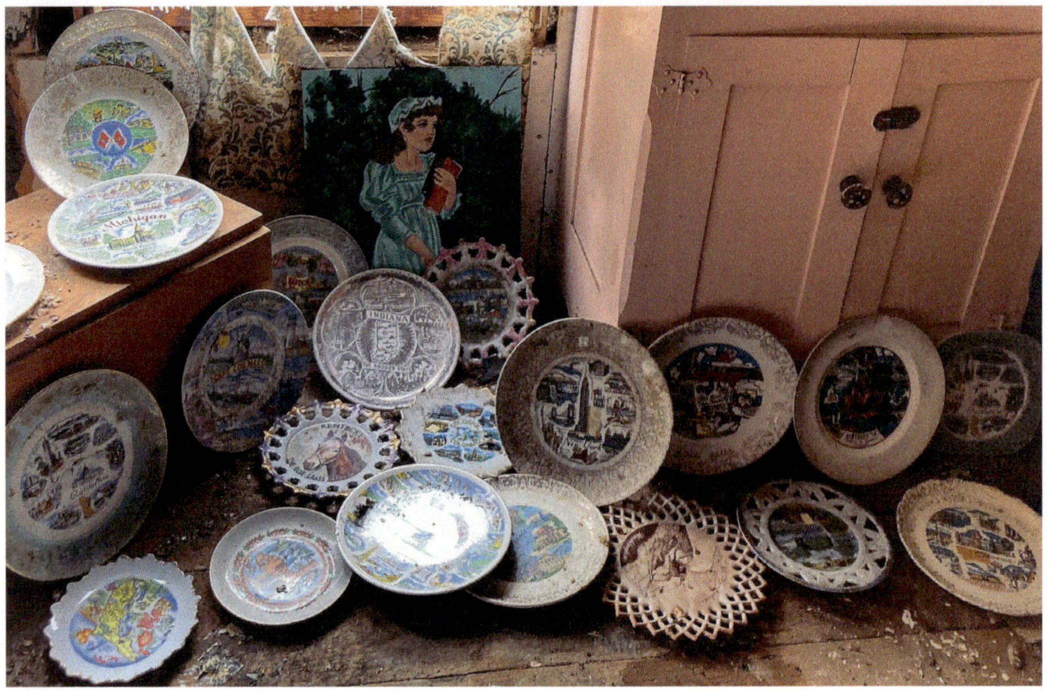

Upstairs in the bedroom, a plethora of plates proudly display the owner's travels, each one a unique souvenir from a different state.

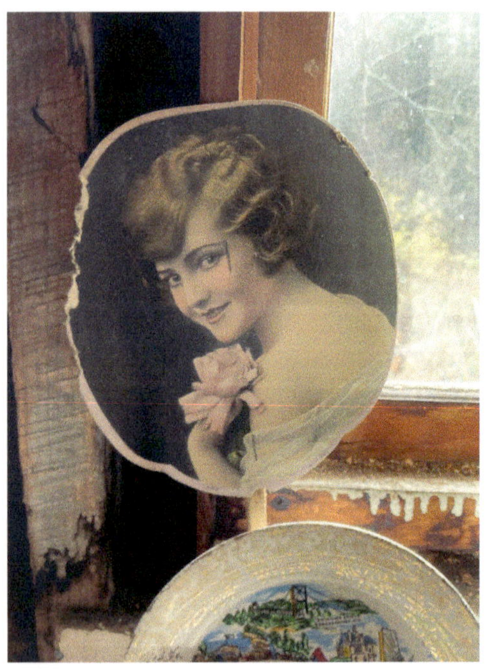

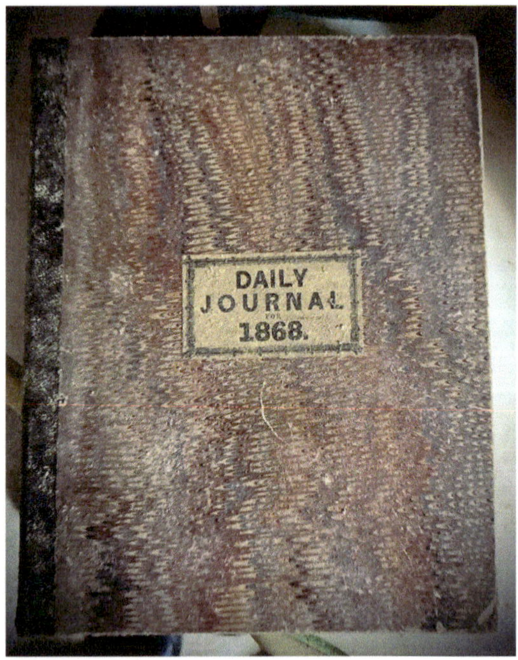

Above left: I thought that this was beautiful and had to take a picture.

Above right: You can expect my excitement when I came across this daily journal from 1868. It's incredible to think about the insight we can gain from someone who lived almost two centuries ago.

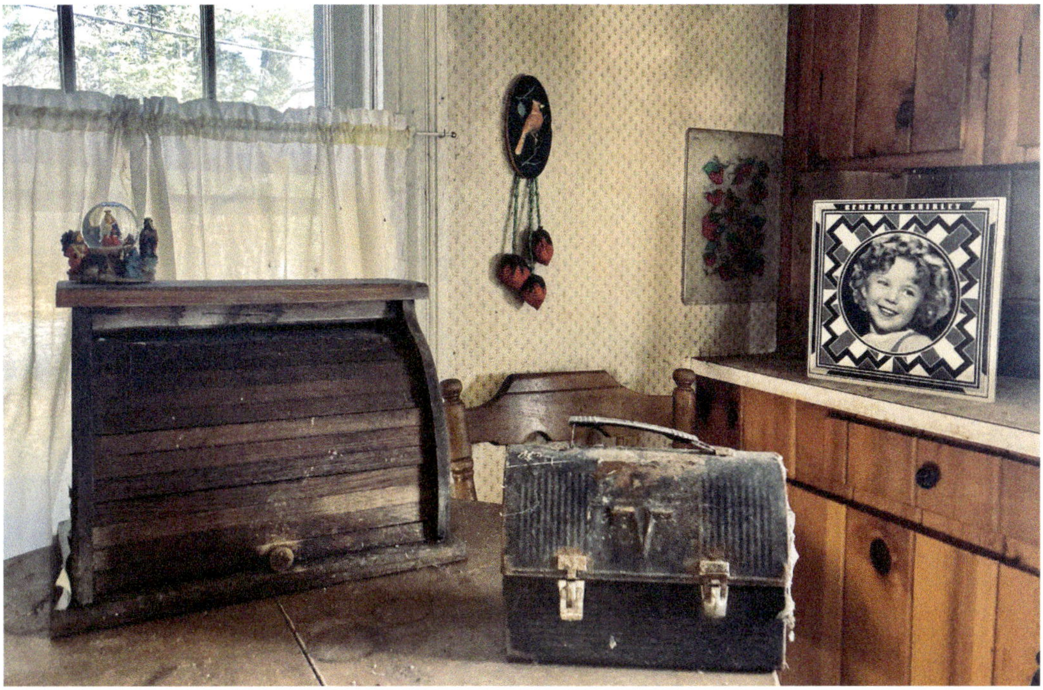

Imagine being able to take yourself back in time. I could picture myself as if I had grown up here, sitting at the table, listening to records play, and waiting for an apple pie to come out of the oven.

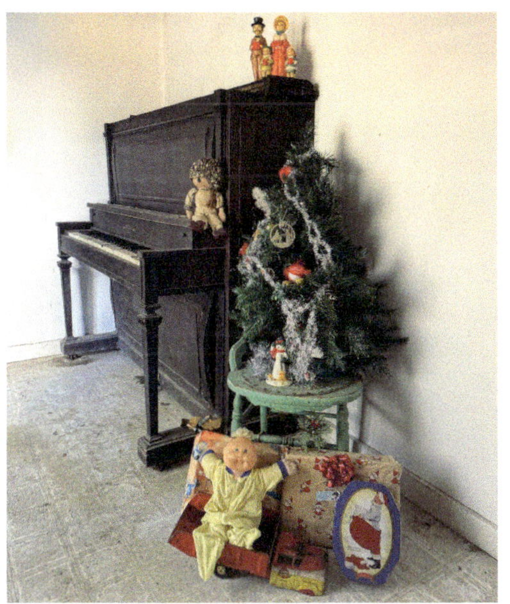

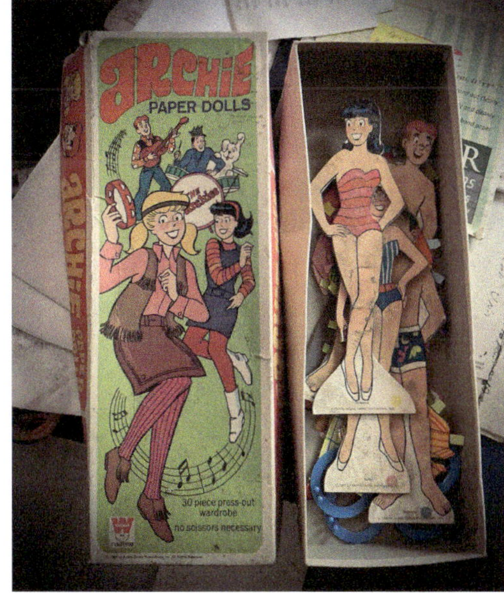

Above left: The handcrafted doll, Cabbage Patch, dump truck, and collection of gifts wrapped and labeled, just for display, all highlight the creativity within this warm and welcoming home.

Above right: These Archie dolls, copyrighted in 1969, were made by Archie Comic Publications. They were an upgrade from earlier versions—made of thin paper—that I found in another room. These, however, were precut. Most families probably found them more convenient and safer for children, since no scissors were needed.

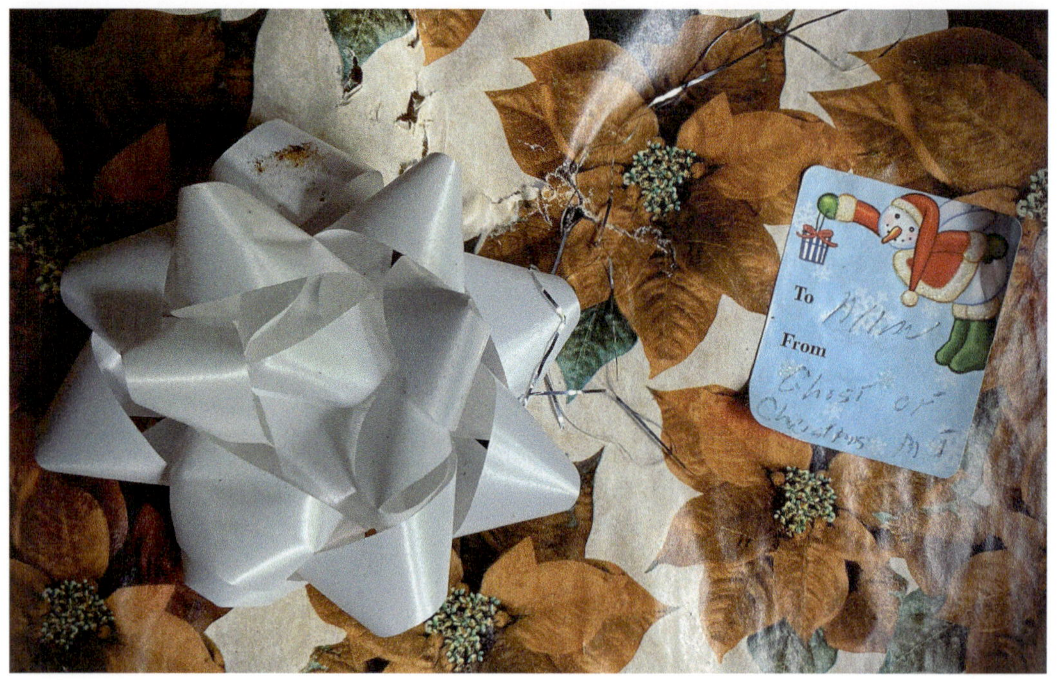

This label cleverly states it's from the "Ghost of Christmas Past."

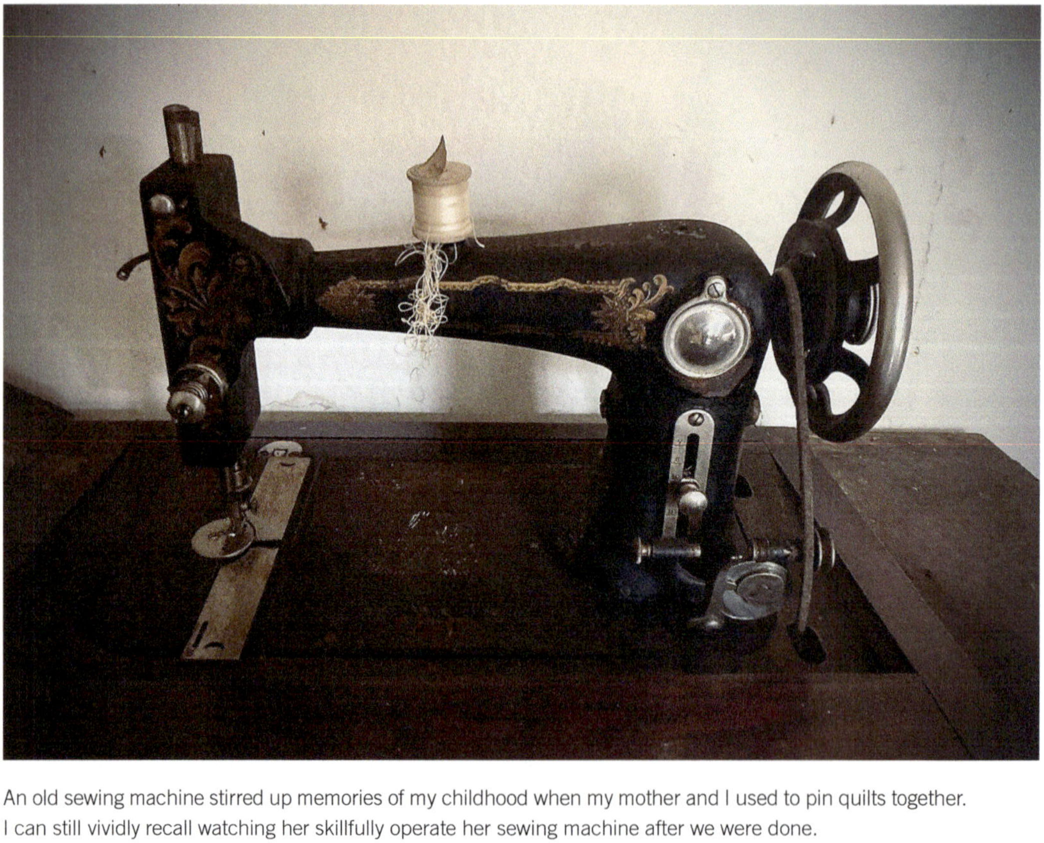

An old sewing machine stirred up memories of my childhood when my mother and I used to pin quilts together. I can still vividly recall watching her skillfully operate her sewing machine after we were done.

2

WHITTIER GRIST MILL

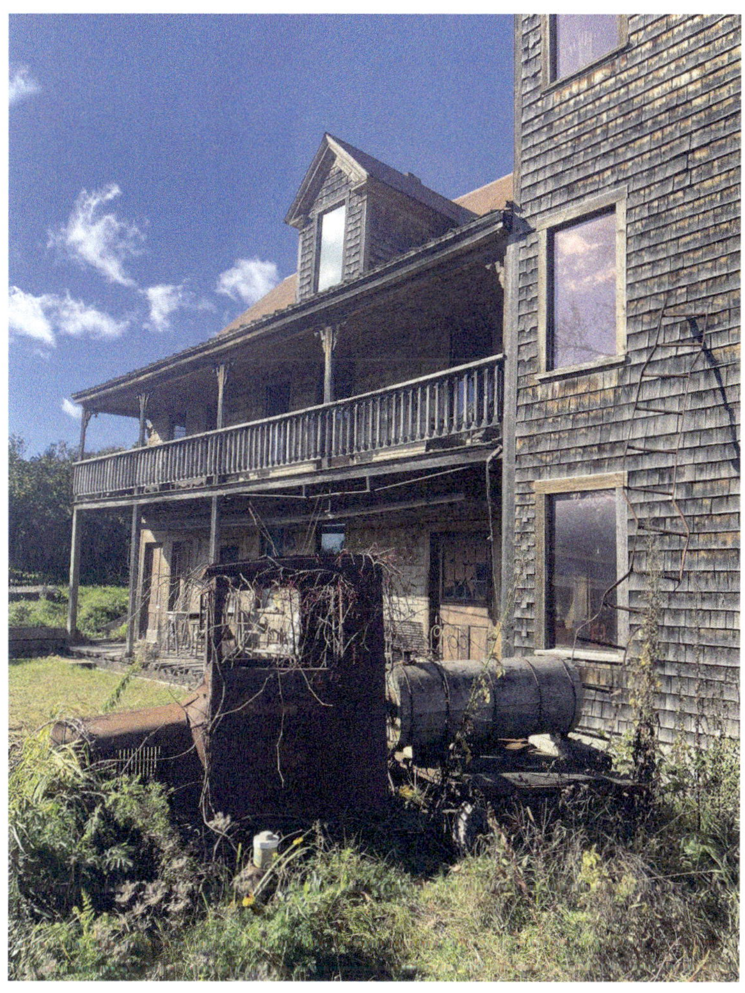

An old grist mill and truck sit dormant, waiting for me to discover its history within.

Dating back to the early 1790s, this Grist Mill was a hub for grinding local corn and grains. Located in Mount Vernon, the village was established by Captain William Whittier, who recognized the untapped potential of the land and its water resources. Whittier purchased all of the surrounding land and built a dam in the village, along with an upper dam at the outlet of Flying Pond. He also established the grist mill, along with a small saw mill adjacent to it. Remarkably, the original machinery still stood within its walls, including the iconic water wheel. This rugged structure stands as a result of extraordinary craftsmanship from a previous generation. Stepping around the building to the rear entrance, I was immediately struck by the breath-taking view of the lake that unfolded before my eyes. Inside, an array of possessions spanning over 200 years could be found, each offering a glimpse of the different eras that shaped its history. From items dating back to the mill's construction in the 1790s to relics left behind by a family that made it their seasonal home in the 1970s, subtle clues from various periods were scattered throughout the building, waiting to be discovered by the keen observer.

The kitchen, with its timeless charm, beckoned me further inside. A hand pump sink immediately caught my attention. Exploring further, I noticed a vintage refrigerator upstairs, complete with a metal ice-cube tray. Then a peculiar sight greeted me to the left: a Styrofoam piece concealing a secret underground door, leading to a set of stairs. The stairs connected the upper and lower floors of the mill, adorned with shag green carpet. Inside, there was a light. The door, cleverly disguised with a pulley system, could easily be overlooked, blending seamlessly with the flooring. Such intriguing features were just the tip of the iceberg in this historical edifice.

The lower level accommodated a second kitchen alongside a bar, where a grand stuffed moose and deer stood guard. An unexpected delight awaited me in the form of a player piano tucked away in the same room. Discovering a player piano was a first for me, sparking my curiosity and fascination. Growing up playing the keyboard, often with my grandmother, and even participating in a piano recital at the tender age of nine, the thought of a piano playing itself was enthralling. It's moments like these, filled with unexpected discoveries and connections to my past, that make each adventure truly special.

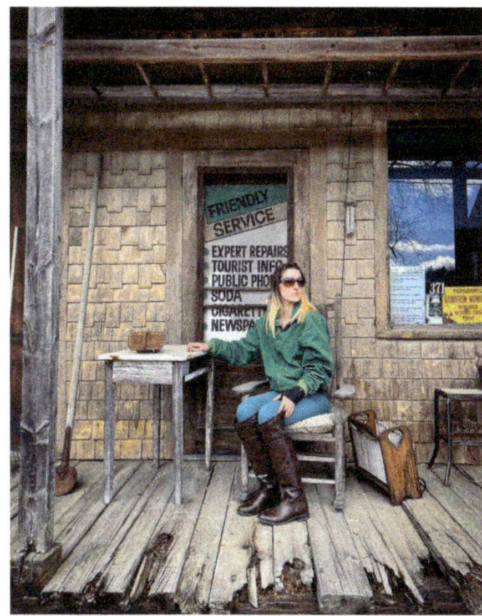

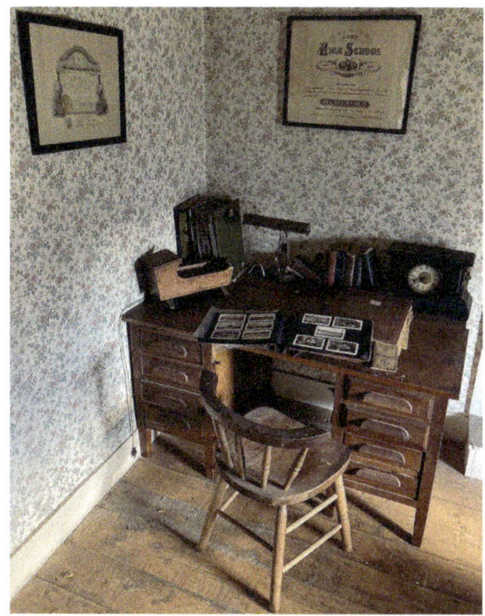

Above left: I paused here for a moment to reflect on what life must have been like back in the day. [*Ally Remillard*]

Above right: Imagine all of the handwritten letters that were penned at this desk. A diploma hangs, framed above.

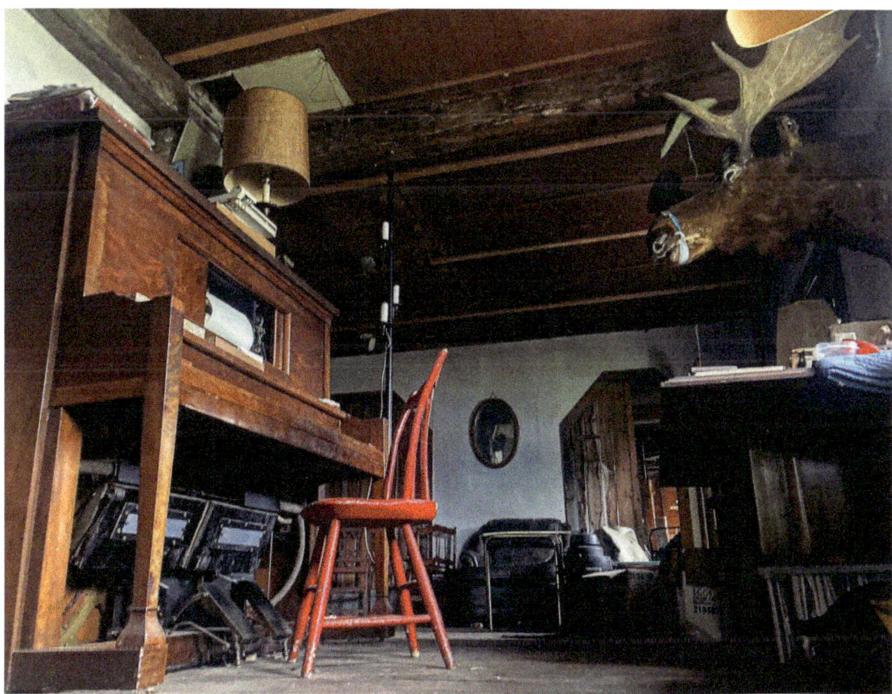

Here sits a player piano. A player piano operates under a mechanism that automatically plays the piano without the need for a human pianist. Alongside it sits a bull moose, one of my favorite discoveries here.

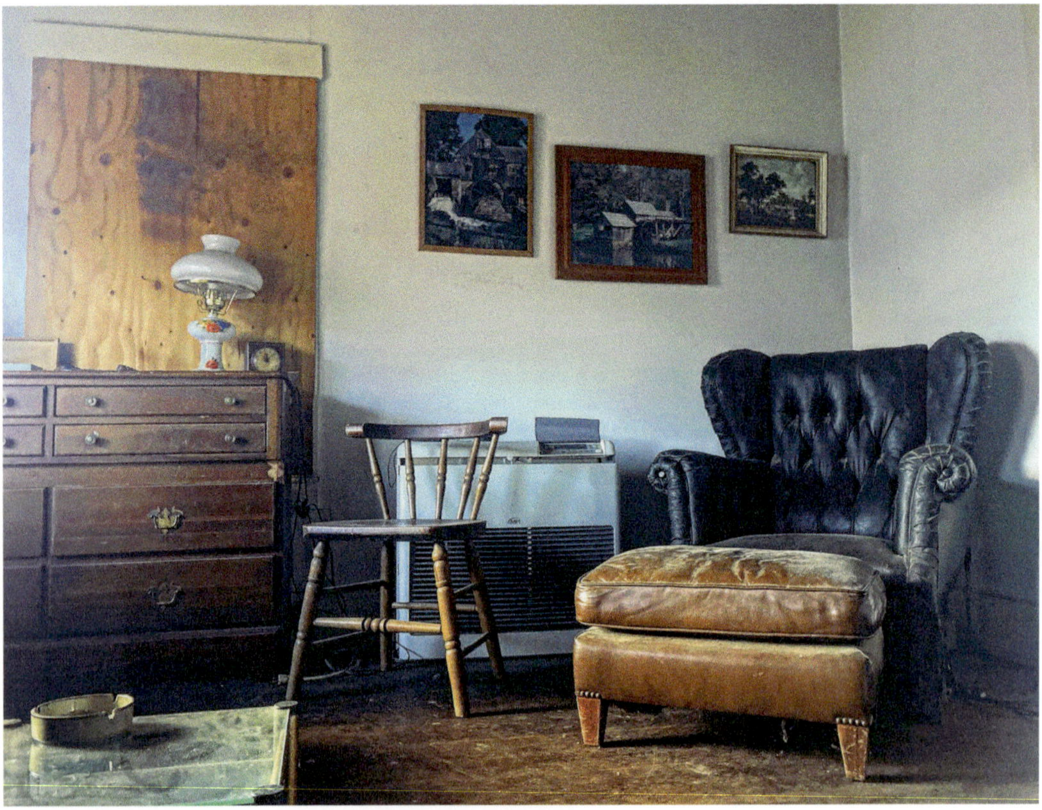

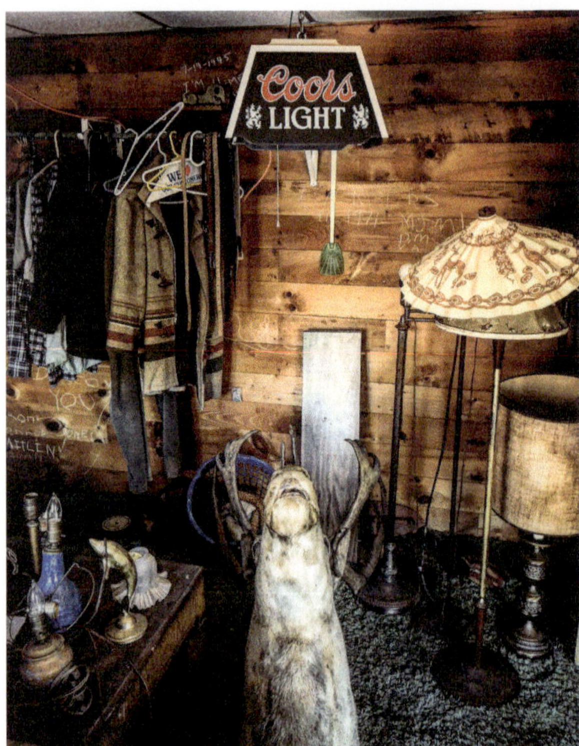

Above: Half of the mill showed evidence of previous living quarters, filled with a unique assortment of furniture.

Left: In this room an elk and its surroundings created a rustic and masculine atmosphere, similar to what one might find in a man cave.

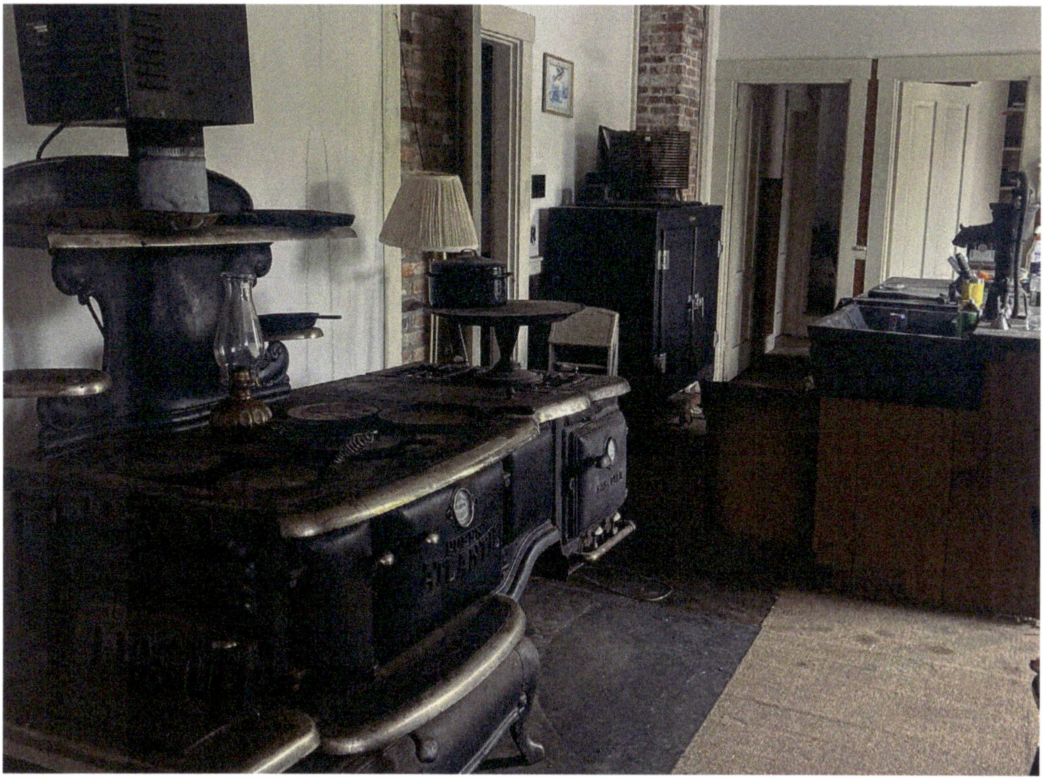

Upon entering the mill, this is what I saw. The kitchen stove, GE fridge, and sink showed me a time when durability was prioritized.

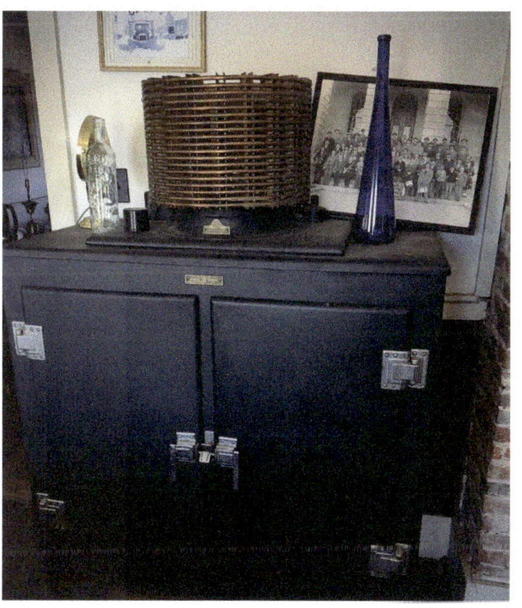

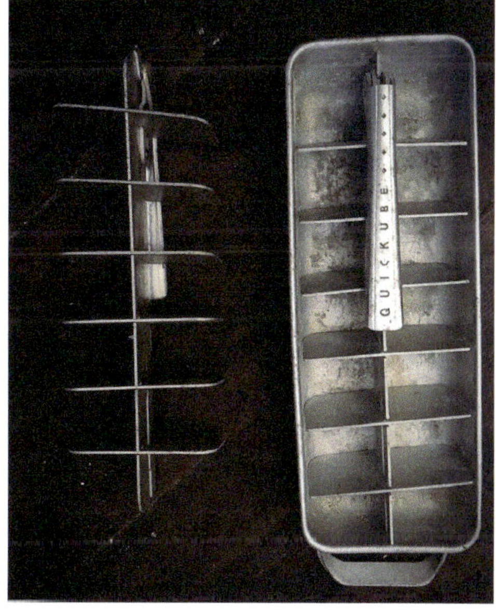

Above left: This GE fridge had an old quickube tray left inside of it.

Above right: This metal tray once held ice; most now are made from plastic.

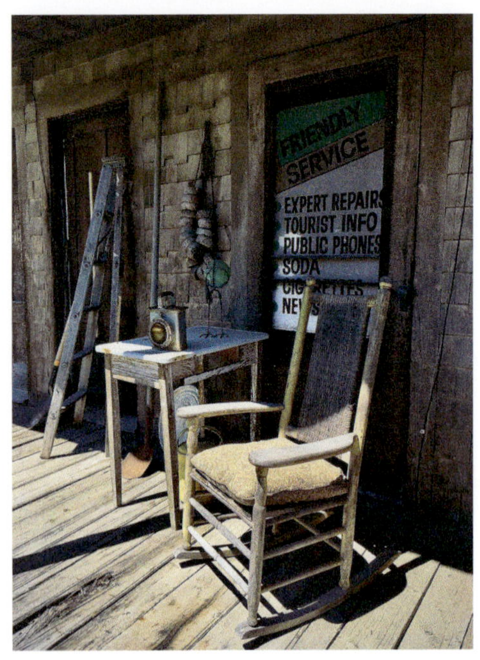

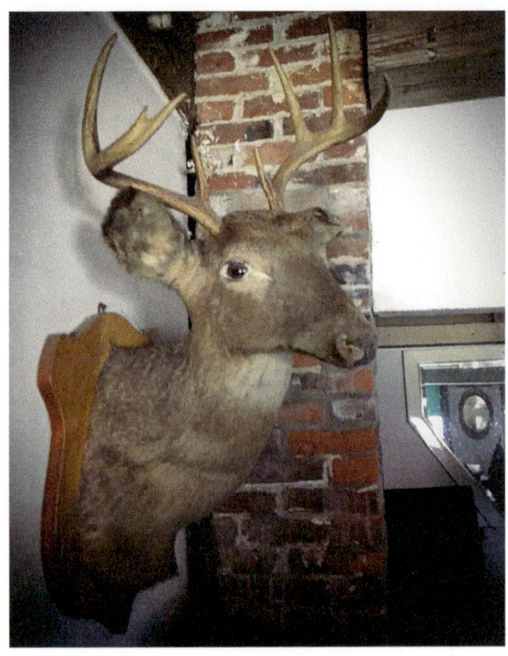

Above left: I love the inviting feeling of this place. The sign saying "Friendly Service" is very welcoming. I bet this mill was once a beautiful sight to see, situated right in the middle of town.
Above right: This deer head shows a time when taxidermy was done differently than it is today.
Below: Whenever I saw this moose, it reminded me of the one at Bugaboo Creek in South Portland where I used to work. Too bad it couldn't talk like the one there used to.

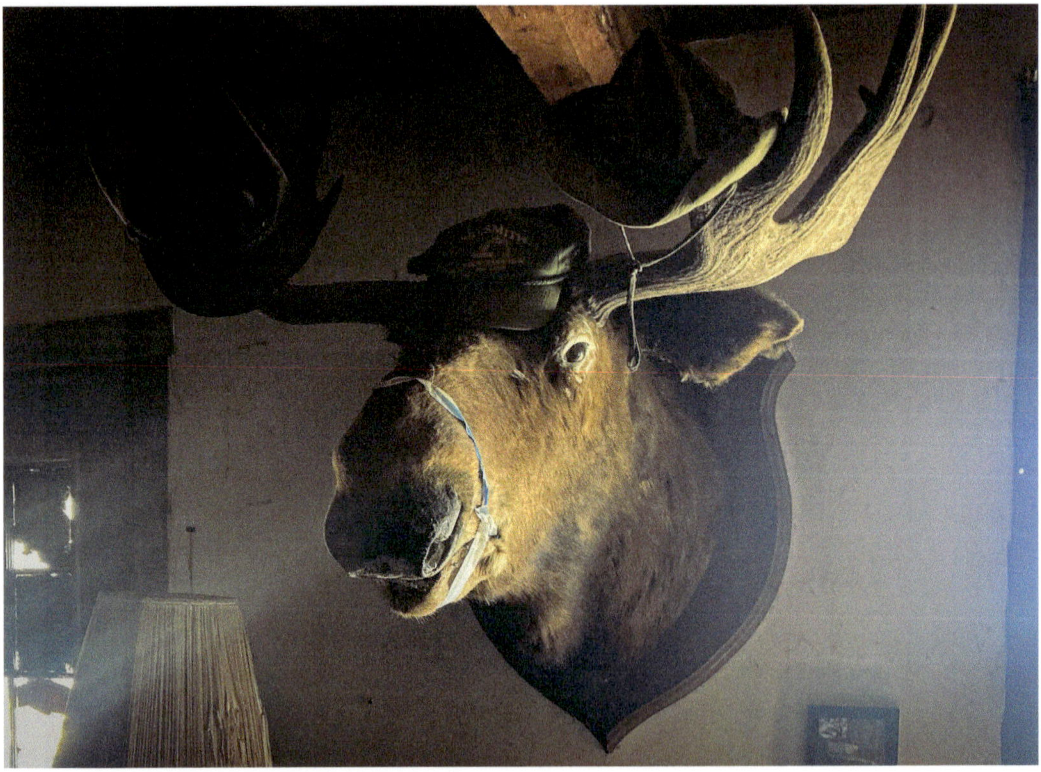

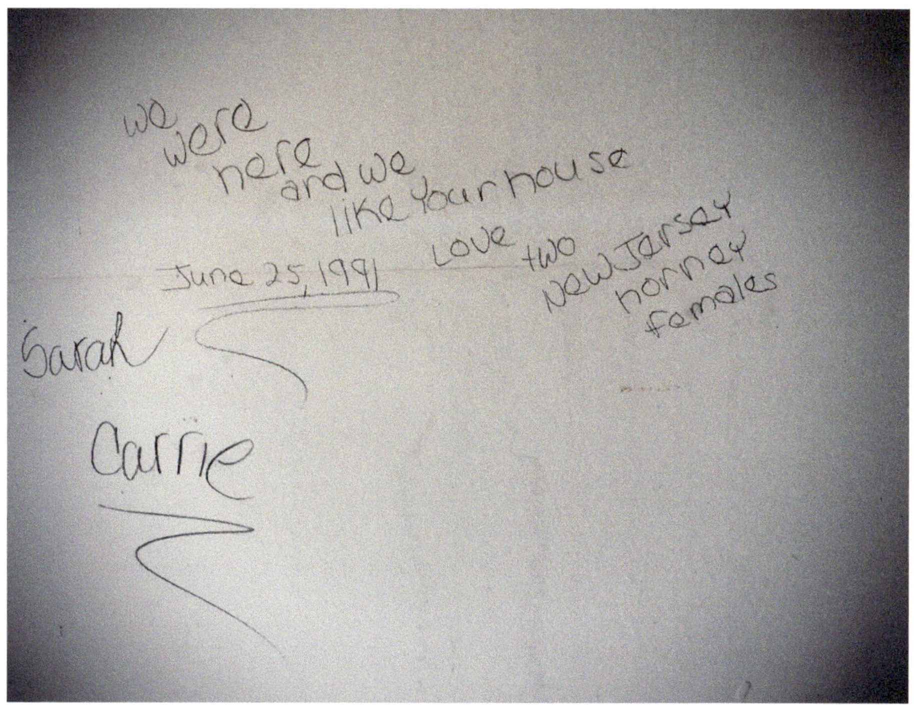

It appears that Sarah and Carrie had a little fun here the year that I was born. When I saw what was written on the wall, I couldn't help but laugh. Previous inscriptions from others date back to 1945 and 1971.

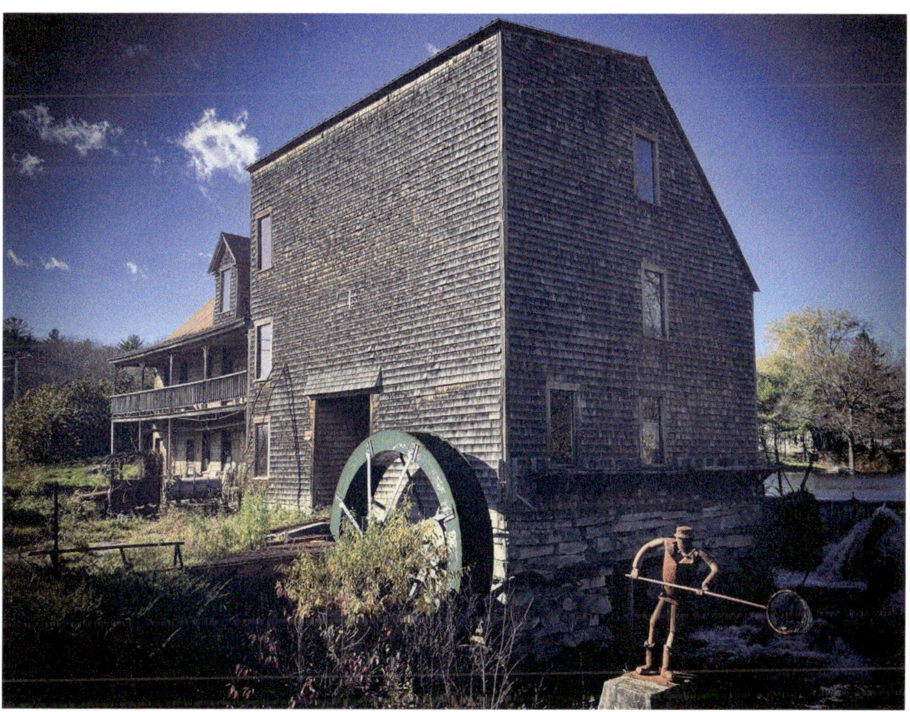

Here, you can observe the mill, along with its water wheel and a distinct piece of art that compliments its setting.

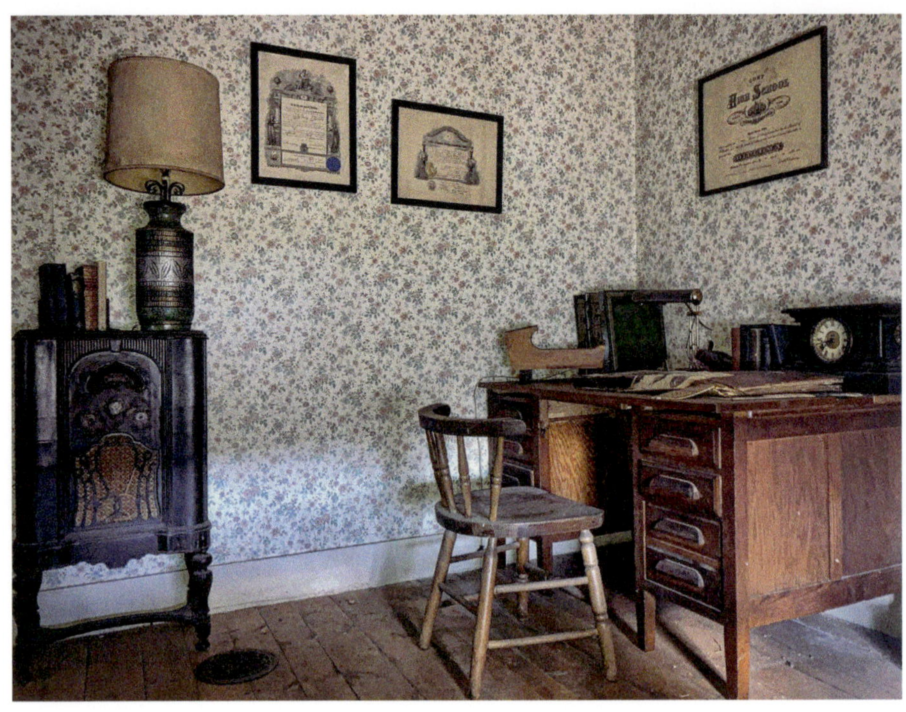

Accompanied by this desk is a beautiful radio, with a stunning lamp sitting on top of it.

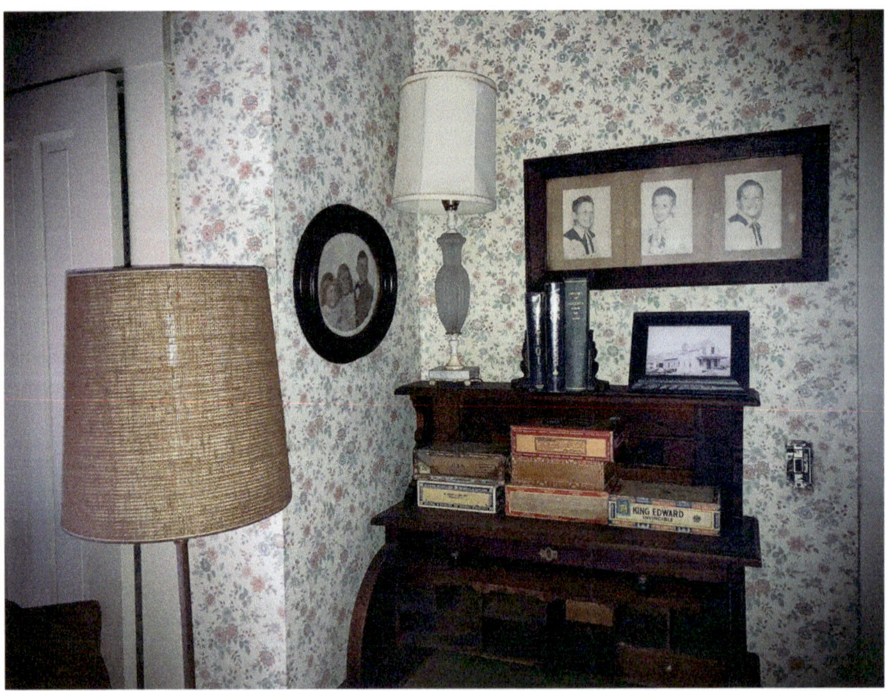

The small picture in the black frame is of the original post office that used to sit on the same side of the road as the mill. The building is still standing, but it's no longer utilized as a post office. Between the two is the old saw mill.

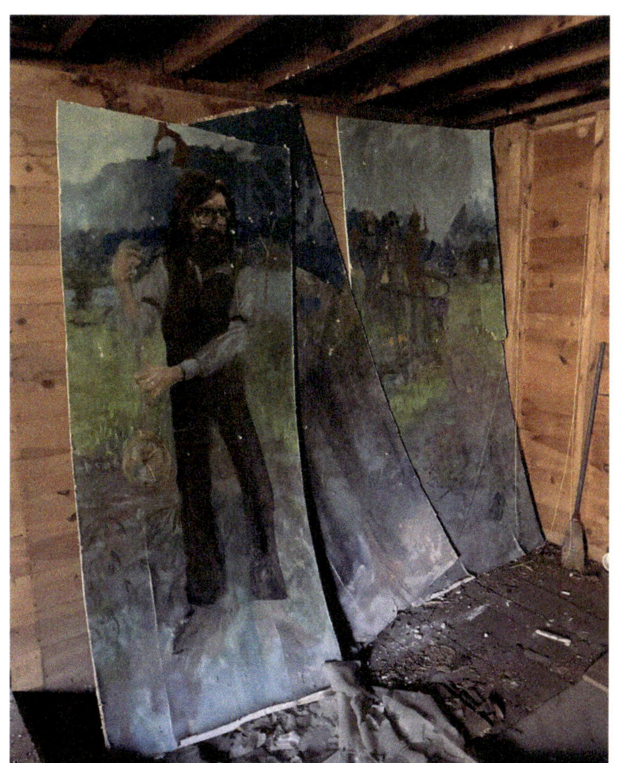

Someone was quite the painter. I couldn't help but capture these lovely paintings. I hope people appreciate my artwork someday, long after I'm gone.

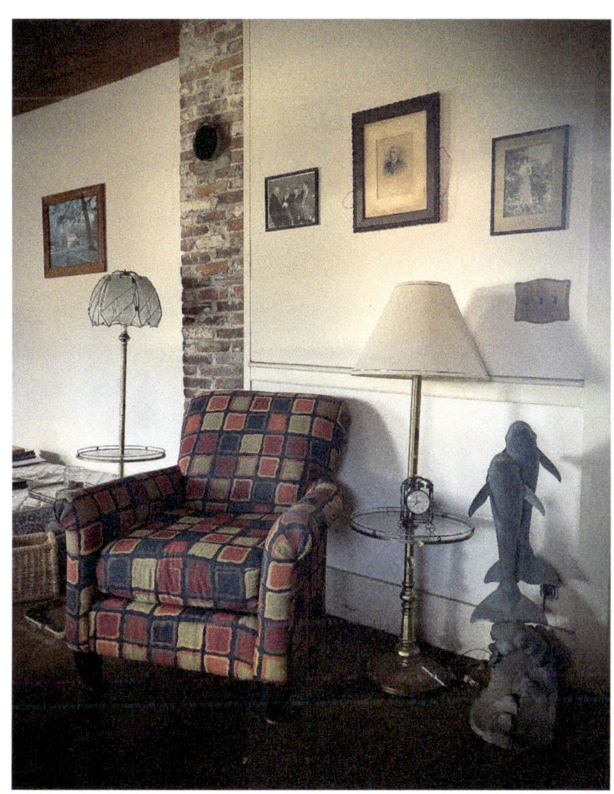

I bet this chair was trendy back in the day. I find the dolphin sculpture to be quite impressive.

3

MAINE'S CHURCHES

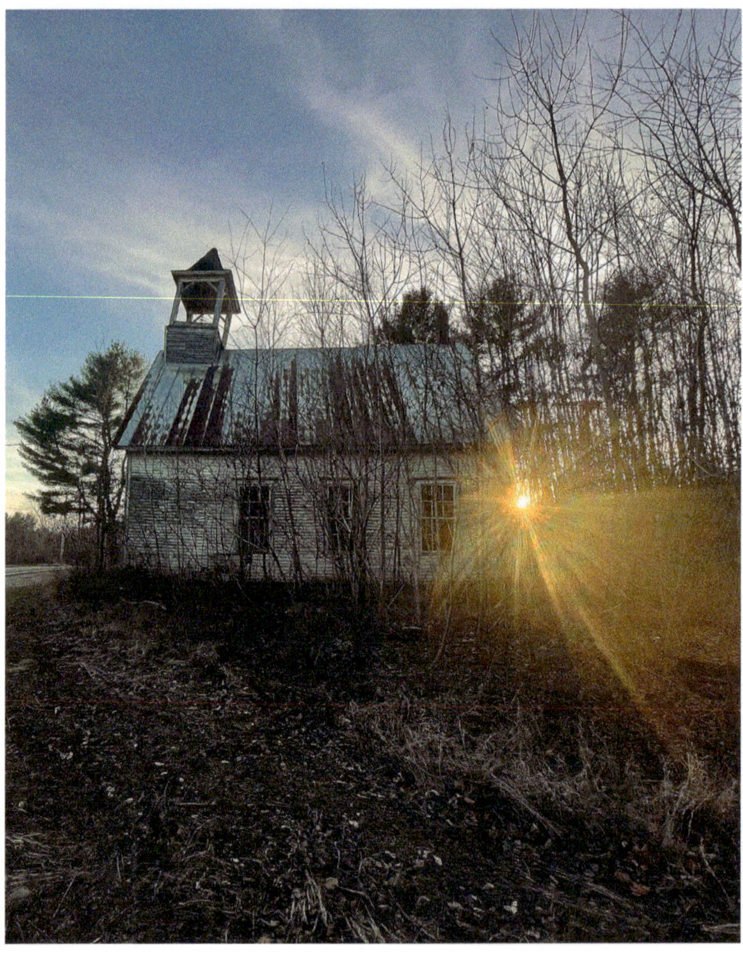

Situated across the street from a cemetery, this church in Washington, Maine, sits right on the side of the road.

Maine's churches initially sprouted up within the towns and communities of the region, many of them constructed from brick or wood. The state was home to a diversity of denominations including Baptists, Methodists, Catholics, Protestants, and more, catering to a population that also included a significant number of non-religious individuals. Meeting Houses were common in many towns, serving as places of worship. Together, it's here that we investigate a selection of churches from the picturesque state of Maine.

East Limington Baptist Church

Perched on a slight elevation off the road, East Limington Baptist Church carries stories of past generations. My mother reminisces about attending church services there and Sunday School in the building next door. The church also hosted the Pioneer Club, a religious themed organization reminiscent of Girl Scouts. Memories include the unique and somewhat eerie incinerator toilets that once frightened my mother as a child. These toilets utilized chemicals to burn waste upon flushing, a feature that could surely spook a young visitor.

The first meeting house was built in North Limington and used as a church until June 7, 1871, when it was struck by lightning. It was damaged so badly that it had to be torn down soon after. For years people from East Limington gathered in North Limington at Ruin Corner, but after the building was razed, a question arose as to

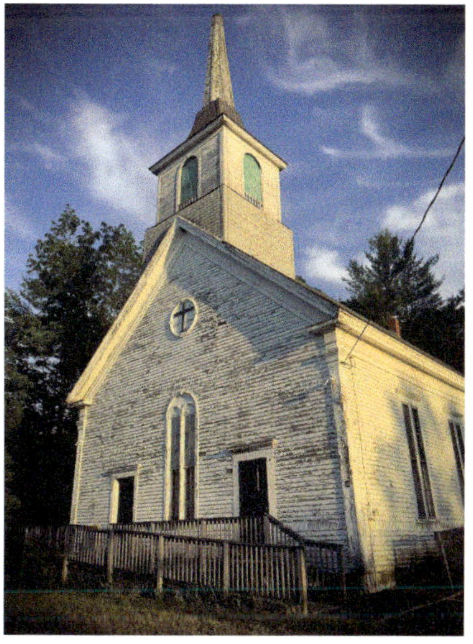

Being raised only a little over twenty minutes from here, I was fascinated to learn about this church's history. I thought it was neat that my mother had visited here as a child.

where the new one would be located. As a result of differences, a division took place within the church. On August 21, 1873, the church was erected and dedicated. At the time, there were thirty-seven members. For a time, the church was called the Calvin Baptist Church, but the church voted to change the name to the East Limington Baptist Church instead.

Cape Jellison Church

In the years leading up to 1947, the community at Cape Jellison felt a need for a Sunday School to cater to the children in the area. A group of dedicated individuals came together that year with the intention of building a church. During this time, lumber was both scarce and costly. However, Reverend Clifford Crabtree, hailing from Bangor, managed to acquire a large barn from Paul Shaver.

The barn was purchased on May 14, 1947, and a lot for the church was secured on May 24. The barn was dismantled, and the finest timbers were utilized. Construction began on June 10, and the project was completed swiftly by August 15. All the funds required for building the church were generously donated through voluntary contributions. The building of the charming church was a collaborative effort, with volunteer workers pouring their time and effort into the project.

It was christened the Full Gospel Lighthouse, and its Sunday school officially commenced on July 20, 1947, under the guidance of Mrs. Clifford Crabtree, with sixty-three children enrolled. The Dedication Service took place on August 17, featuring a sermon by Clifford Crabtree and a prayer led by Reverend Otis R. Barber from Roxbury, Massachusetts.

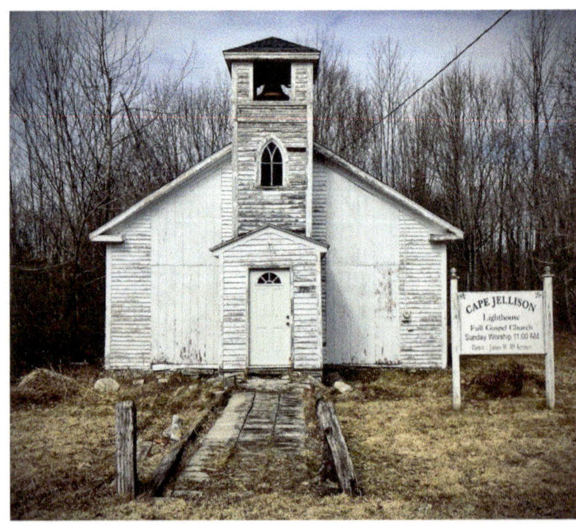

The bell remains perched in the tower. I should have investigated to see if there was a rope attached to it.

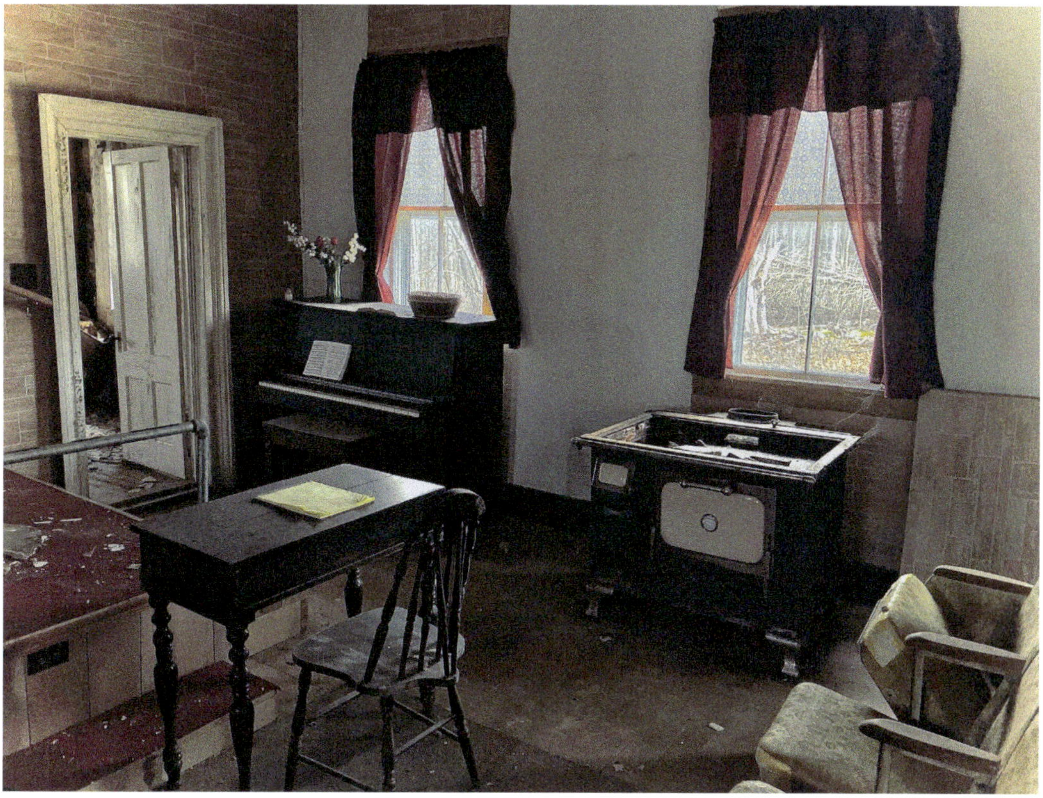

Inside the church, there were two pianos. I identified an old stove next to one of them, serving as a reminder of the days when it was used for heating.

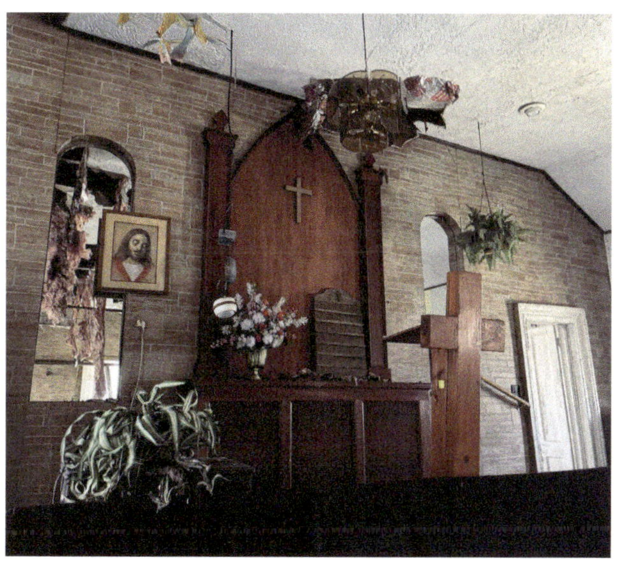

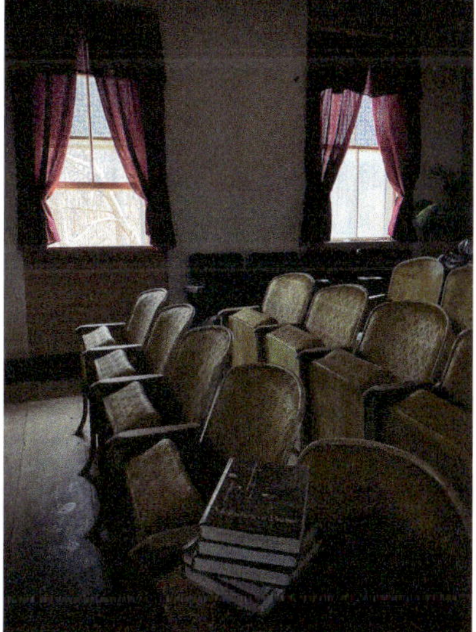

Above left: The exquisitely crafted wooden cross podium stands proudly, complementing the cross positioned behind it. The artificial plants further enhance the ambience of this space.

Above right: Hymns were left behind, destined to remain untouched.

Newburg, Maine Church

Established in 1878, this church in Newburg, Maine, stands as a non-denominational sanctuary that once served as a shared space for various congregations. As economic prosperity grew and resources became more accessible, individual denominations were able to construct their own meeting houses.

Before 1906, Maine was mainly characterized by Methodist, Baptist, Adventist, and Catholic faiths. However, during the significant outpouring of the Holy Ghost at Azusa Street in Los Angeles, California, the flames of Pentecostalism ignited and spread rapidly, reaching even the state of Maine. In 1906, the first touch of the Holy Ghost was felt at this old Calvinistic Baptist Church in Newburgh, Maine, known as "The Newburgh Center Union Society," where Brother Harry Woods served as the pastor. As people fervently prayed for the salvation of their loved ones, the Holy Ghost descended upon them, filling them with its power, causing them to speak in unknown tongues. This divine encounter was so profound that even passersby in wagons on the road outside the church were moved to repentance and prayer by the Holy Ghost's conviction.

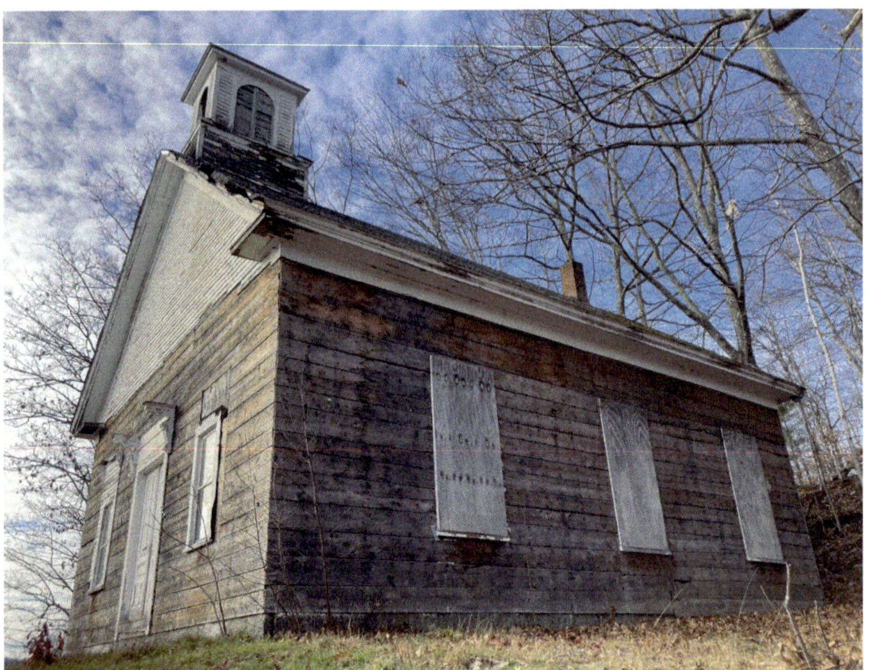

As I passed by this enchanting wooden church, I was astonished to find it was wide open on the other side. Not much remained. Inside there were a of couple chairs, an old wood stove, and the rope from the bell tower still hung, offering a glimpse into a different era.

In the quaint village of Newburgh, the church became a focal point for these spiritual manifestations. The flames of the Holy Ghost soon spread to Southern Maine, leading the Newburgh church to adopt a Pentecostal identity and be known as the "Newburgh Center Pentecostal Church" post-1906. Prior to 1917, there weren't any Pentecostal churches north of Bangor.

Central Maine Church

Built in 1906, this church in Central Maine has a haunting past that transformed a once loving community into a place of morbidity. After being decommissioned as a Methodist church, it fell into the hands of an owner who resided in the building with a large horde of cats. Tragically, the owner passed away and was discovered six months later, having been partially consumed by his feline companions. Rumors swirled about a neighboring individual who attempted to renovate the church after the owner's demise, only to meet a similar fate in the basement, where their body remained undiscovered for three months.

During an exploration of the church, my friend and I happened upon a deceased cat inside, adding to the horror. The fate of the cat left behind remains a mystery. With a little research I discovered concerned neighbors had shared stories about seeing a cat in a window, on social media during the COVID-19 pandemic. Were the rest of the cats freed once their owner was discovered deceased? It seems likely. Perhaps this particular feline was simply concealed, escaping the notice of the authorities, unknowingly abandoned, now just like the church. My friend and I covered up the poor cat with its owner's shirt and said a prayer. Being mostly made up of bones and dust at this point, we tried to provide it with some peace, as best as we knew how.

The idea of entering the property for most seems daunting. On a separate trip, a cop told my friend to leave because it was haunted. Instead of telling her directly, he told her friend at the vehicle where they were parked, asking to pass the message along. He refused to go inside. The police officer then left and did not investigate any further.

The church itself bore witness to neglect, with overflowing cat boxes and abandoned toys scattered throughout. Ironically, this place of worship was known for celebrating Halloween as a playful holiday for children, hosting a haunted house and distributing candy unlike most. Little did the town know that one day, the church would become a real haunted house, leaving a lingering sense of creepiness in the community.

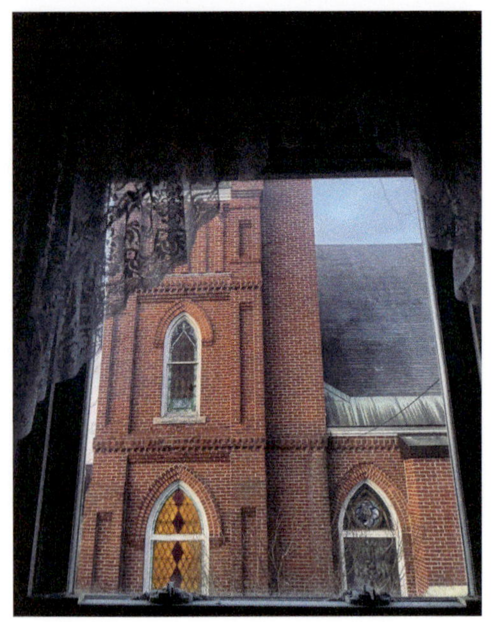

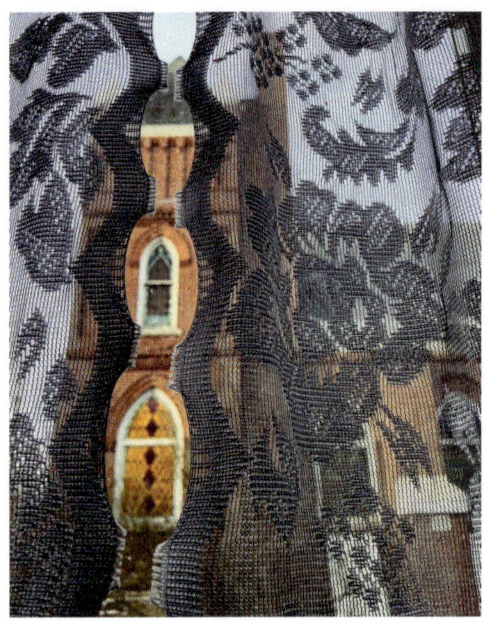

Above left: This image was taken inside the parsonage adjacent to the church, highlighting a creative way to be in two places at once and illustrating the interconnectedness of both locations.

Above right: In this shot, I aimed to capture the delicate lace curtains framing the windows of the church, showcasing a unique and artistic approach to photography.

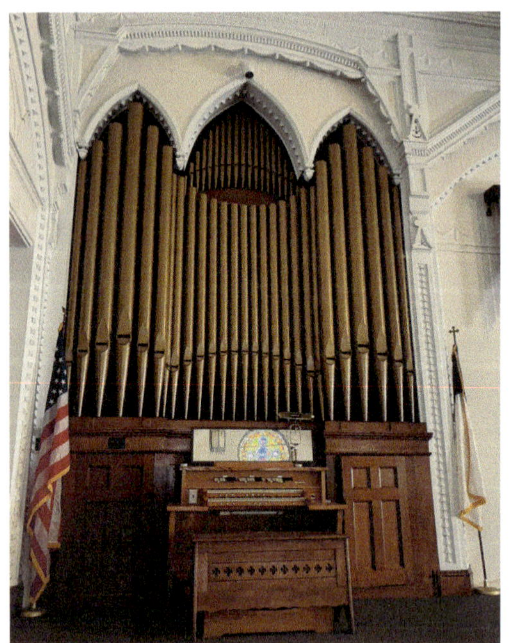

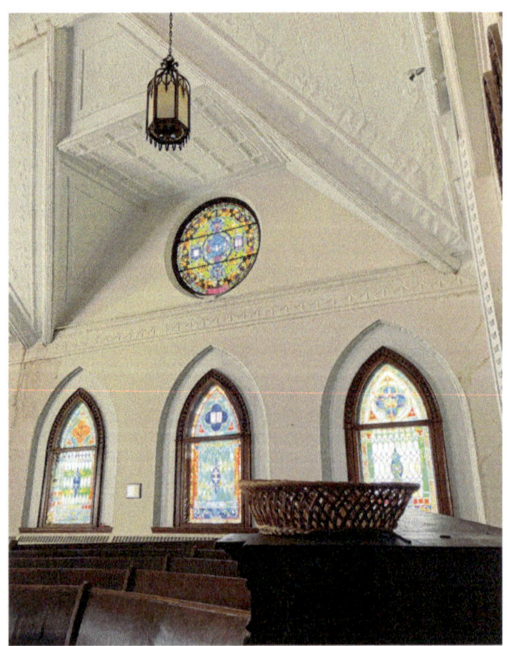

Above left: The pipe organ sits un-played, where it has been for a number of years.

Above right: The offering basket remains untouched, a quiet witness to neglect and a reminder of the church's past vitality.

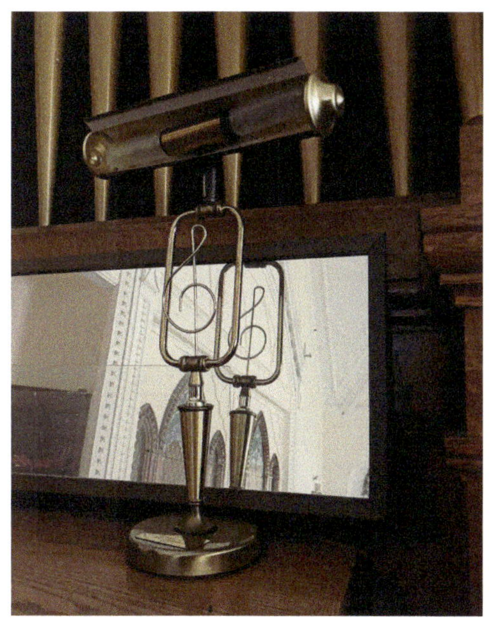

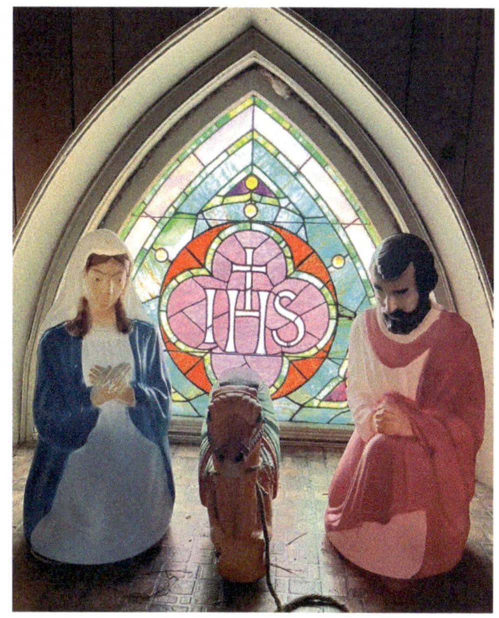

Above left: The light, intricately designed with a treble clef in the center, sat perched on top of the organ, creating a beautiful focal point.

Above right: Upstairs, toward the rear of the Sunday school area, decorations and supplies were stored.

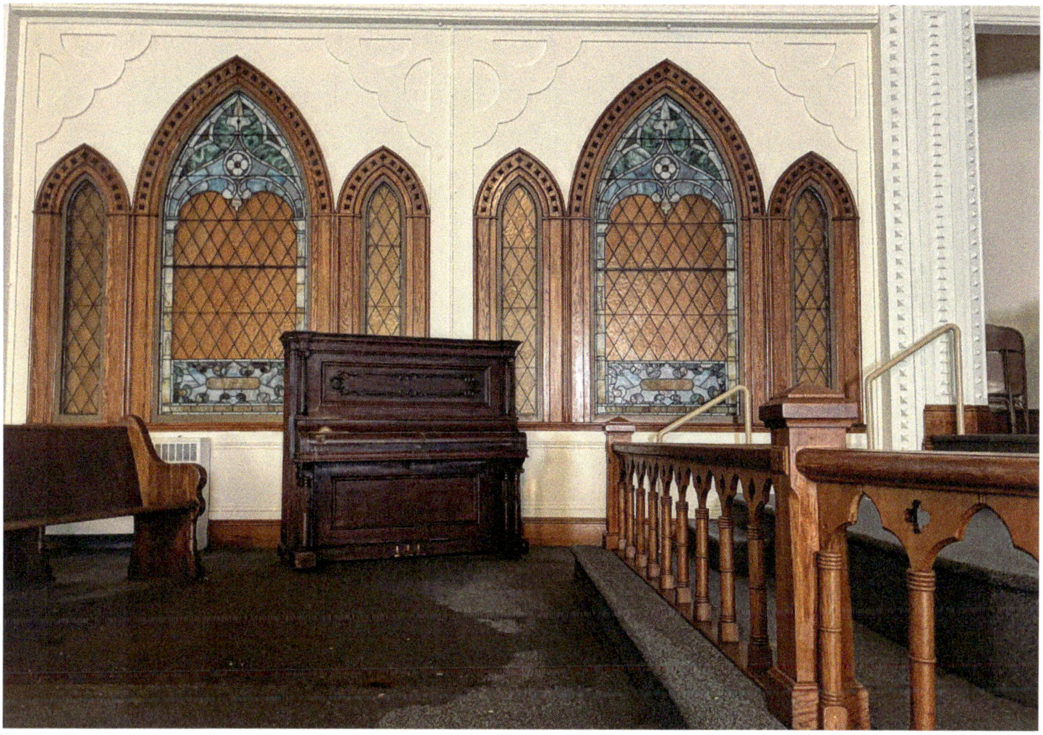

The church pews now deserted; the floor marred by water damage.

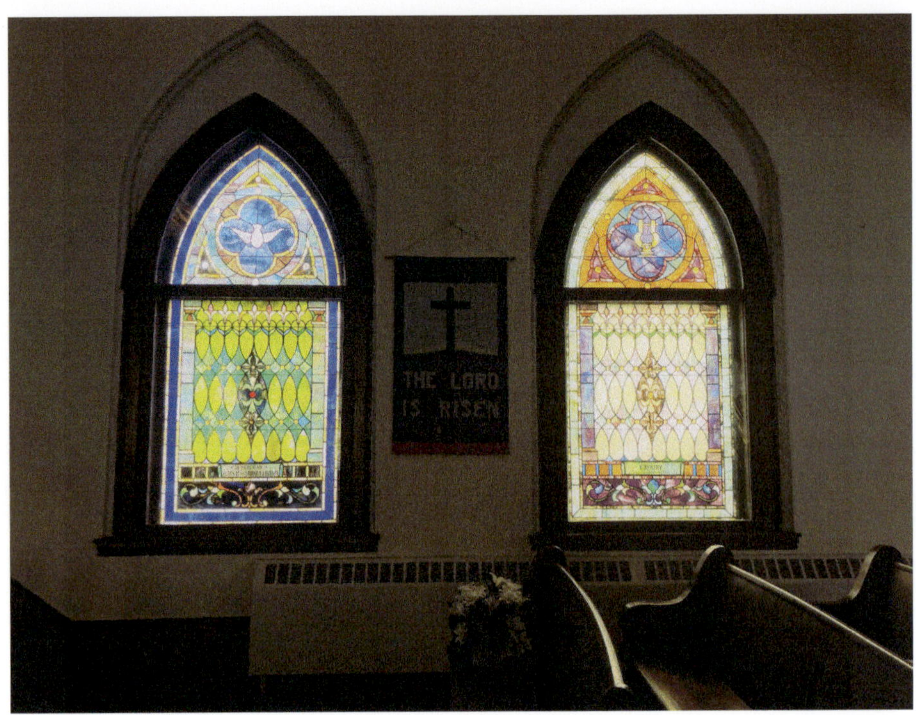

The stained-glass windows in this church were dedicated to several individuals. It is remarkable how these windows have stood the test of time.

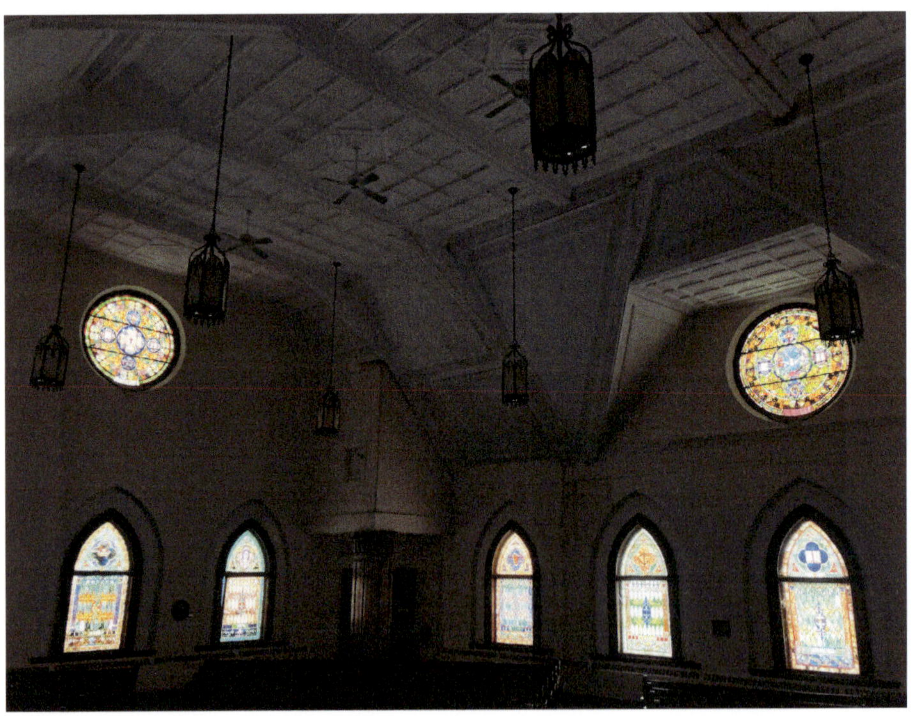

The lanterns hang in perfect harmony with the stained glass, showcasing their enduring craftsmanship.

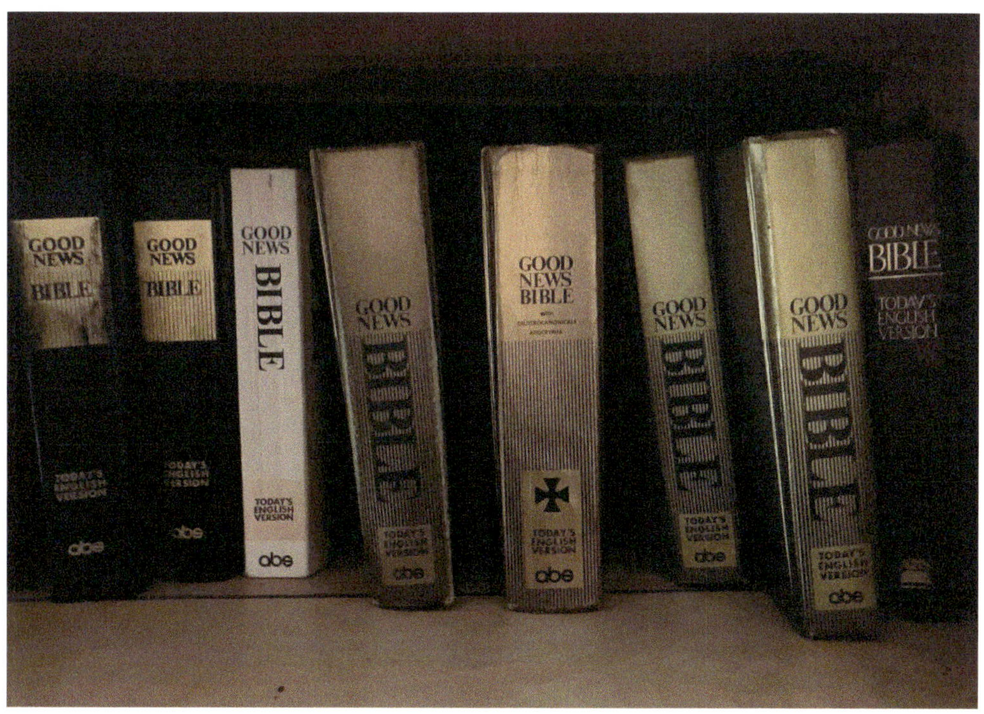

The bibles sit there, perfectly arranged, slowly deteriorating.

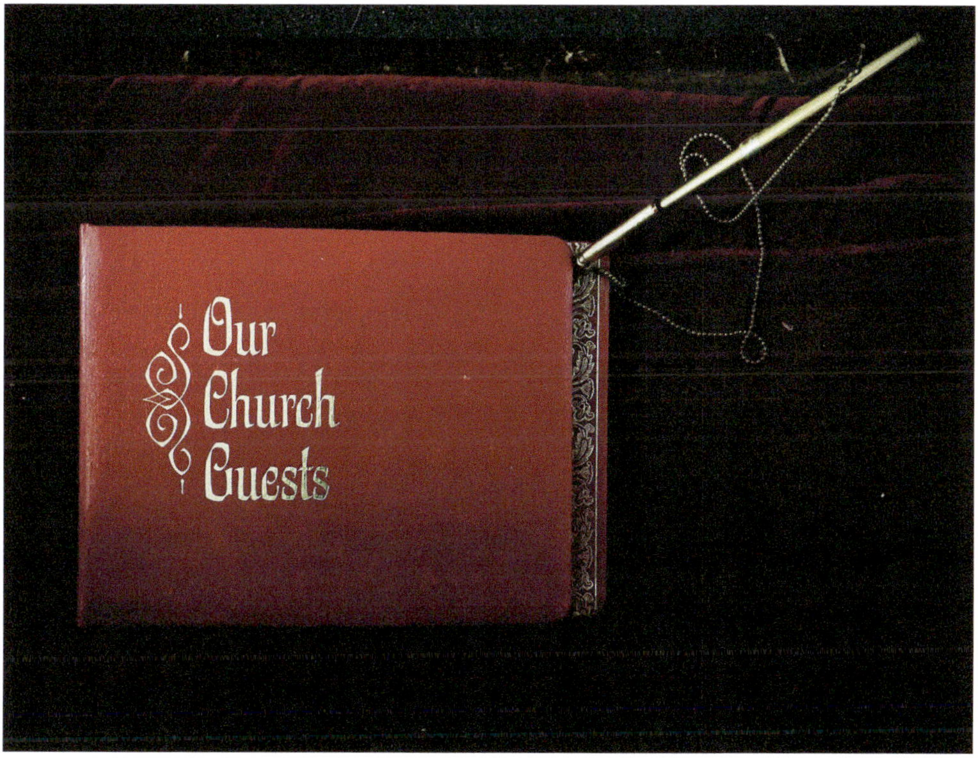

Our Church Guests

The church guestbook stands as a testimony to a livelier time when it was brimming with people.

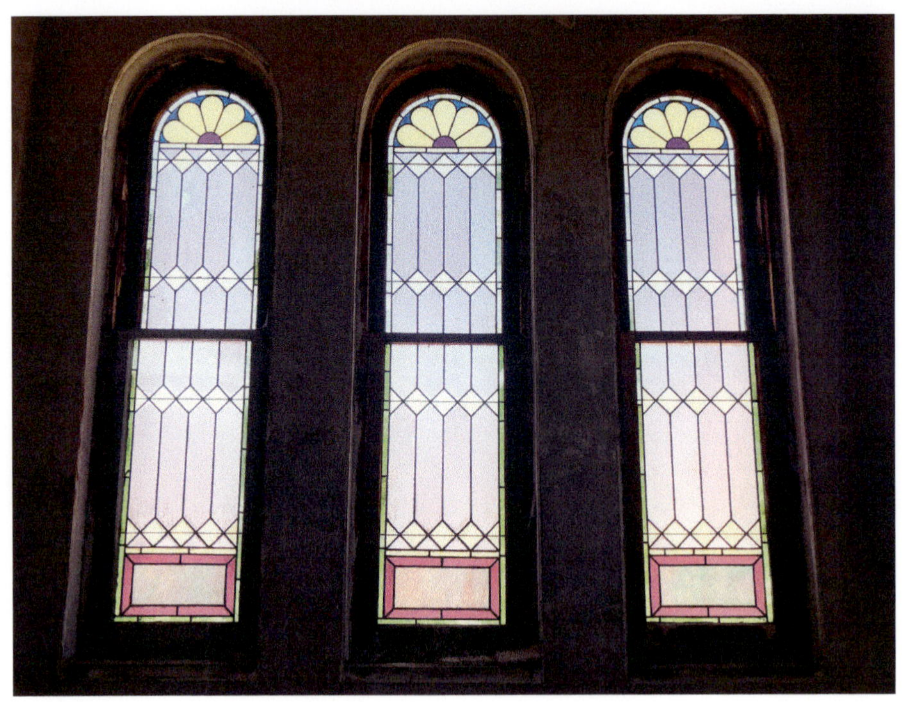

I found the sunlight filtering through the windows to be truly majestic.

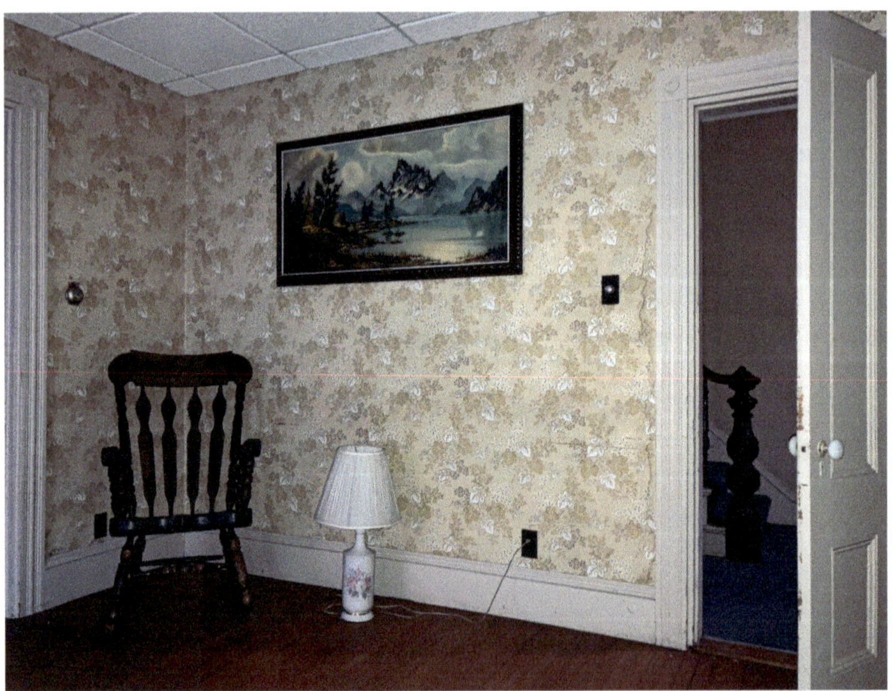

Here is a glimpse inside the parsonage located next to the church. A parsonage was usually provided by the church for its pastor, minister, or priest to reside in.

Washington, Maine, Church

Located in Washington, Maine, stands an abandoned church situated across from an old cemetery, where a headstone has been displaced to the front door. I contacted the town to have it returned to its original resting place, offering my help. The church was eventually sold and repurposed as an auto shop. Locals recall a time when the back lot was filled with numerous cars, adding to the rich history of this now-deserted place of worship.

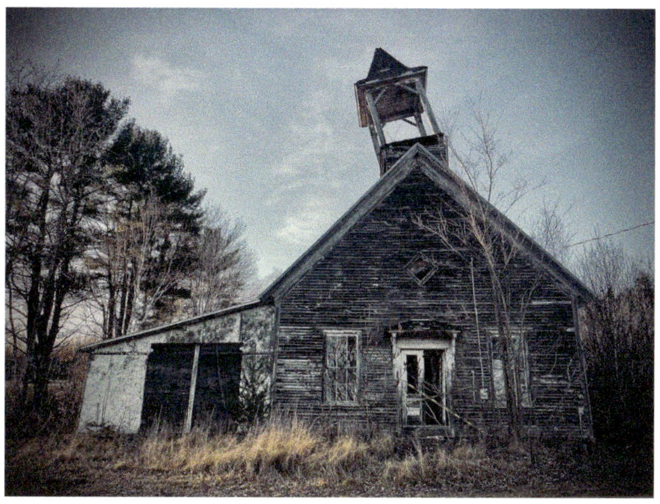

The caution tape stretched across the door creates a sense of danger, evoking an eerie atmosphere that may remind some of a Halloween attraction.

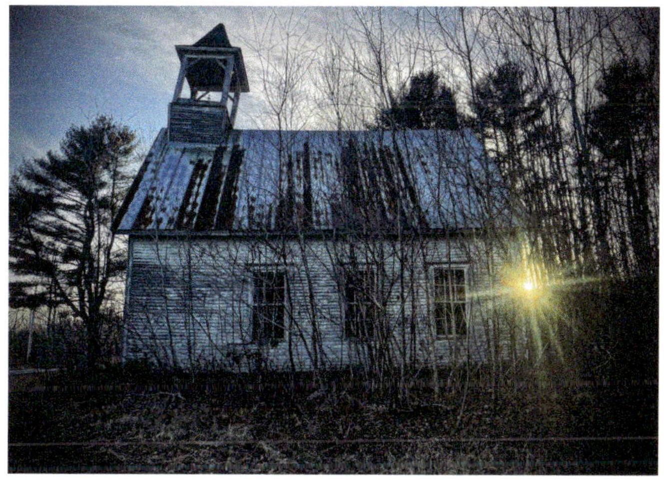

Currently, the only remaining source of warmth here, both physically and emotionally, comes from the sunlight.

Free Will Baptist Church

Constructed around 1845 by the community of New Sharon, this building served as a Union Meetinghouse, with a strong presence of the Free Will Baptist denomination. New Sharon was home to four Free Will Baptist societies, with this being the inaugural one established. Situated just a short distance from an old cemetery, this meetinghouse once held a historical and religious significance in the town.

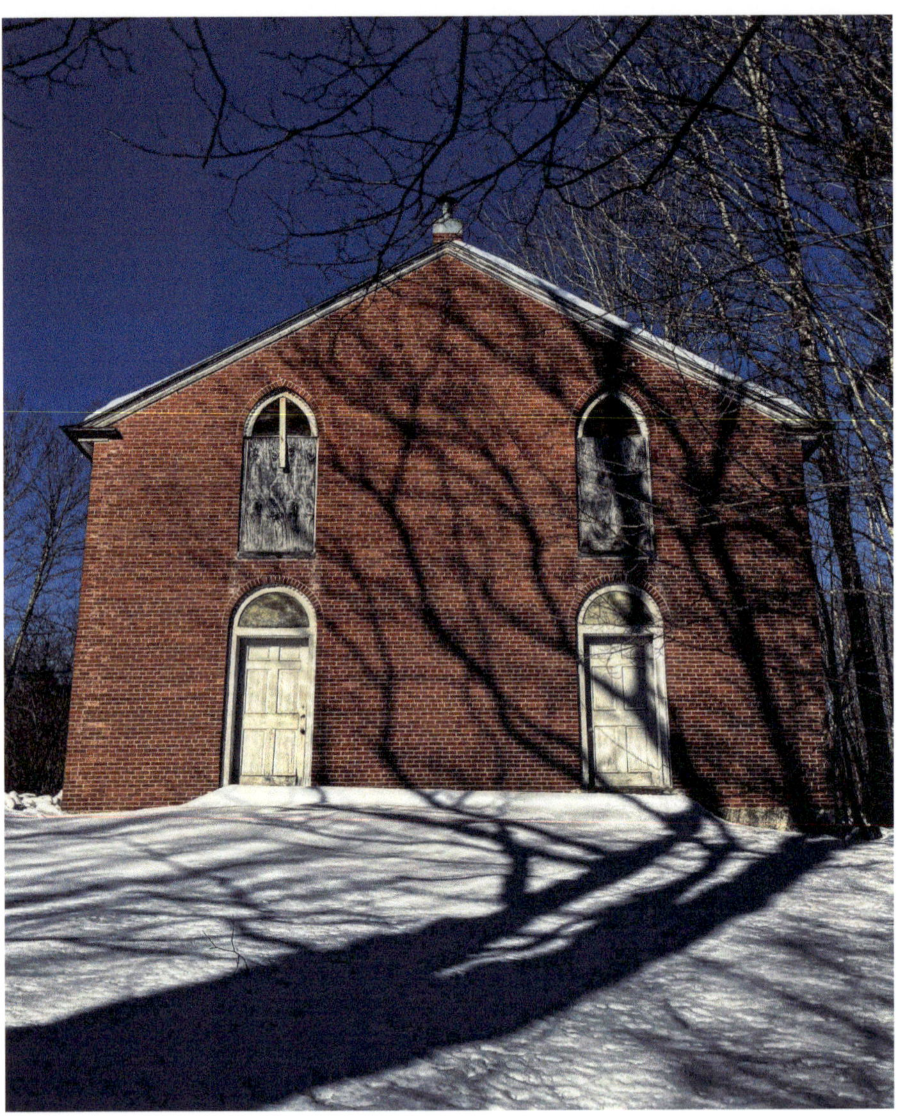

The contrast of white snow, shaded trees, and their reflection against the brick church creates a scene of unmatched beauty.

4

THE TITANIC OF MAINE

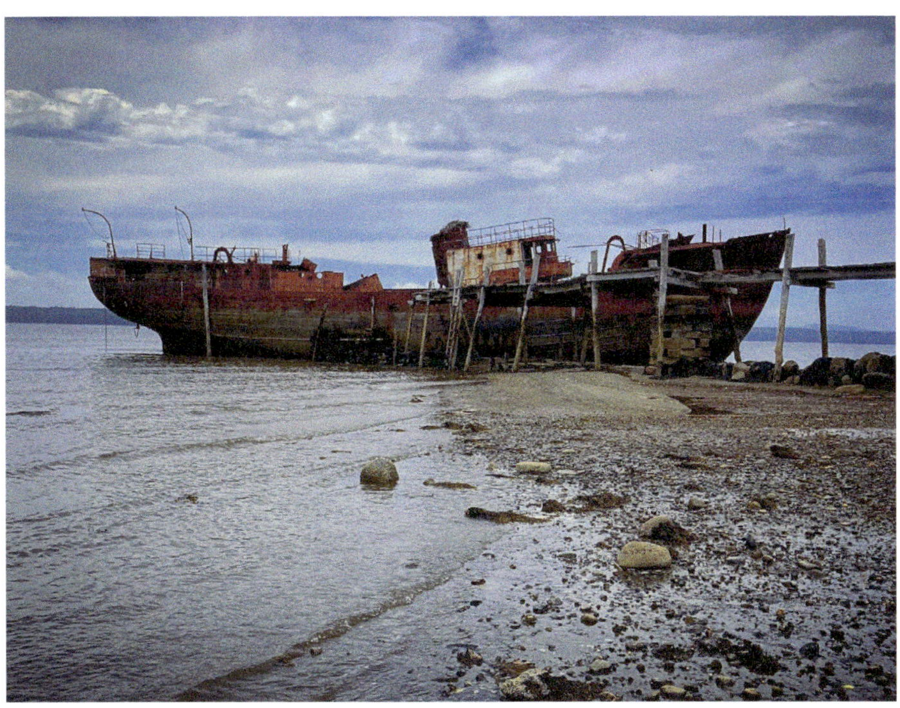

This boat was built in February of 1937, by Bath Iron Works.

In February of 1937, Bath Iron Works built a vessel for the Bay State Fishing Company, originally named FV *Tide*, to be used as a beam trawler. This boat was one of six vessels commissioned for them by Bath Iron Works. In 1938, the General Seafood Corporation acquired this patrol craft from its original owners, changing its name to FV *Squall*. It was equipped with a McIntosh & Seymour Diesel engine, a single propeller, and had a power of 750 shp. Interestingly, my boyfriend, who worked at BIW for nearly five years, gained insight into the modern shipbuilding industry during his time there.

Acquired by the Navy in May of 1942, the *Squall* was shortly commissioned by July that same year. During World War II, the boat, now known as USS *YP-414*, served as a vital asset in contributing to various missions and operations that were crucial to the war effort. Additionally, the USS *YP-414* was awarded the American Campaign Medal and the World War II Victory Medal for its service.

In August of 1945, *YP-414* was decommissioned at Quincy Dry Dock and Yacht. After the war the boat was given back to General Seafood Company where it was used for fishing out of Rockland. National Sea Products, a Canadian company, purchased General Seafoods in 1956. The trawler continued fishing out of Rockland, catching ocean perch for National Sea Products. In 1974, the company phased out its operations and sold off its fleet. By 1977, the boat was beached at the entrance of Morse Cove in Penobscot Bay. It was there that it would reach its final destination and be repurposed as a breakwater for the marina located in the cove.

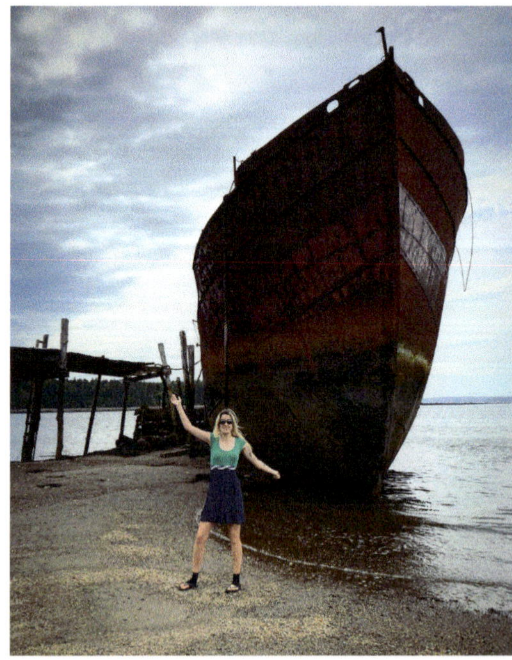

This boat is enormous compared to me. [*Dale Peaslee Jr.*]

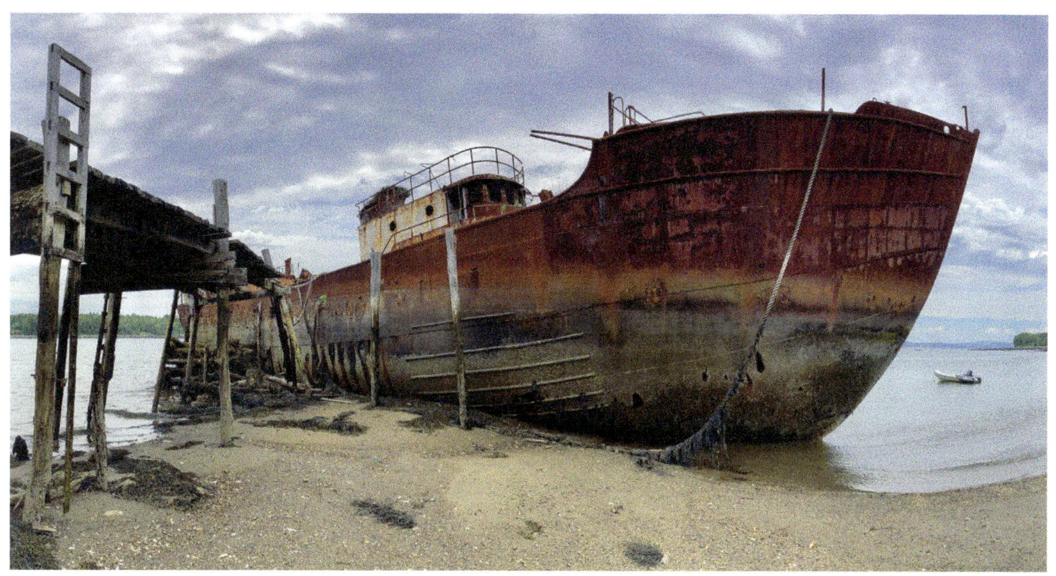

In January 2020, before the Covid-19 pandemic, my boyfriend took me to see this deserted ship. It was a time when the world was about to undergo a significant transformation.

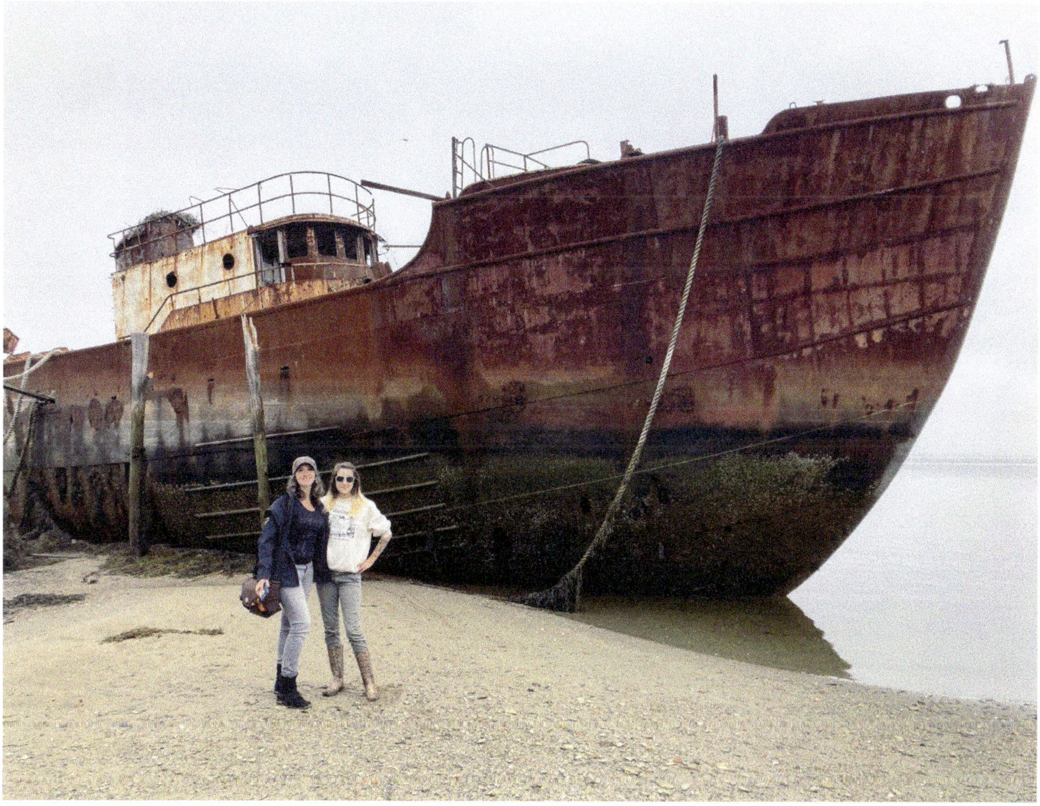

Sometimes strangers from out of state become friends who you invite to sleep at your house, so you can go exploring together the next day. [*Dale Peaslee Jr.*]

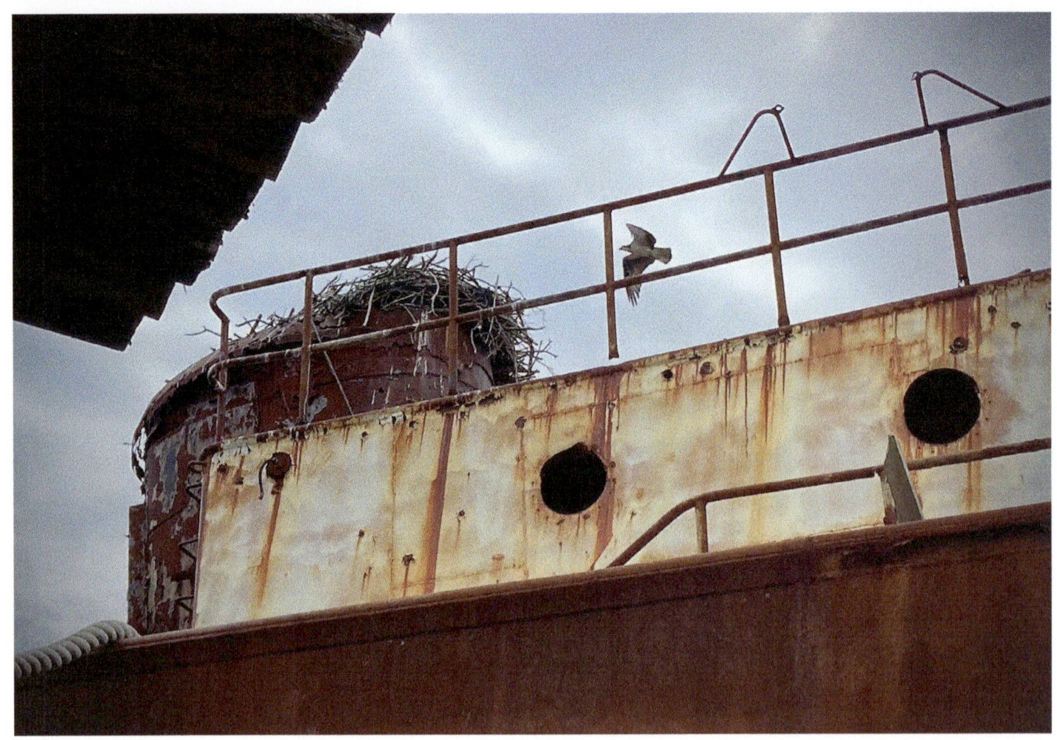

Here is an osprey returning back to its nest. I guess the boat isn't completely abandoned anymore. It seems to continue to be repurposed, now for the birds.

5

BIG SQUAW SKI RESORT

At the end of a lengthy, twisting dirt road sat an abandoned ski slope and a dilapidated resort that was opened in 1963. Dedicated on December 28 by Governor John Reed, it debuted only four trails utilizing a T Bar and a rope tow. The ski area, once thriving with activity, now lay dormant, its equipment scattered about. Green ski benches, matching the building's paint, were left lined up in the grass. Inside the control room, notes, labeled buttons, and old gear painted a picture of a booming business now lost to time and decay. As I wandered through, it felt as though everyone had suddenly vanished, never to return.

Within the vast expanse of the deserted resort, hundreds of skis and boots lay scattered, casting an eerie atmosphere. The building, with its multiple sleeping rooms and communal lodge, exuded a sense of being watched. Upon entering through a wide-open side door, I noticed a cash register on the floor, surrounded by skis. This triggered memories of my youth spent helping my mother at her quilt shop where she had a cash register that looked just like it. A blank room with white walls held two vintage coke machines frozen in time, chilling me to the bone in the freezing weather that day.

Walking through the kitchen, filled with dishware, my nerves were unsettled by the empty, upright freezers that were all located in one room. It ignited dark thoughts of getting trapped inside. I was amazed by everything left. If taken care of properly, a lot of blankets and miscellaneous items could have been donated to a homeless shelter.

After passing a small bar, I ascended the red-carpeted stairs, navigating between floors which felt like following a maze. The decor upstairs evoked a lost era, reminiscent of a scene from *Dirty Dancing*, with a sophisticated dining room adorned with a piano

Exploring down the hallway led me to various bedrooms, each unique yet familiar in layout and bedding. In one room, a neatly turned-down bed bore a note from a young child to their absent mother, surrounded by stuffed animals and a beheaded glass doll, adding to the creepy ambiance. The thought of encountering someone lingered in my mind as I tiptoed through the rooms, slowly rounding each corner.

Over the years, the ski area changed hands multiple times, with James Confalone acquiring the lease in 1995 and initiating renovations that later stalled. The decline continued, marked by a ski lift accident in 2004 and the resort's final winter in 2009. Scrutiny led to the resort's name being deemed offensive, prompting a change to Big Mountain Ski Area, erasing a part of its Native American history. Despite the controversies, the previous owner either staunchly or stubbornly defended the original name, emphasizing its connection to Native American heritage. The resort closed for good in 2010. As of 2024, part of the mountain has been reopened for skiing. There is now a Bombardier snowcat that'll bring you to the top, where the resort still sits, abandoned.

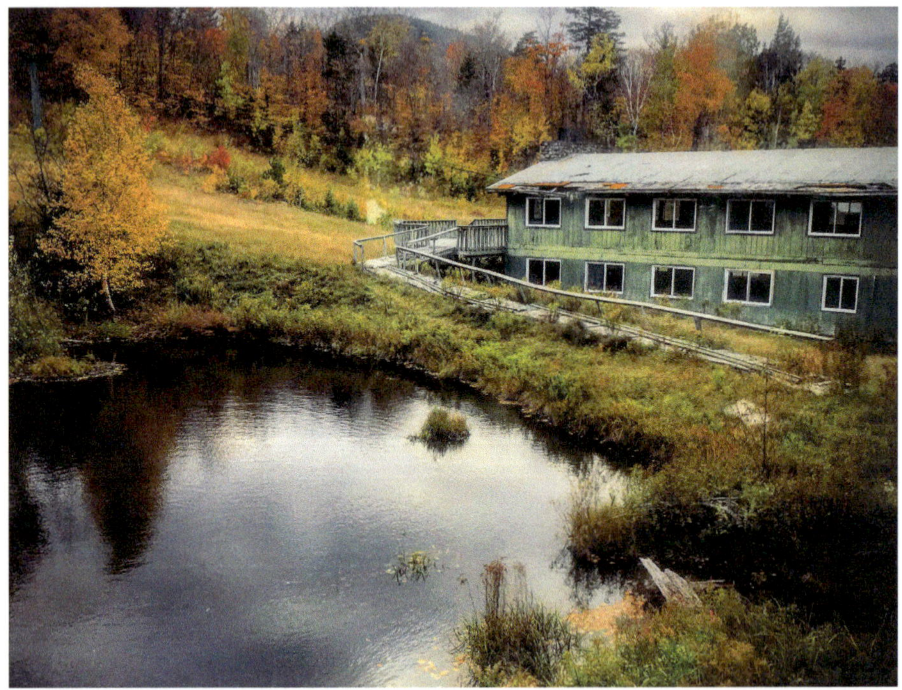

For years, the primary visitors to this resort were wildlife, passing through. Now, part of the mountaintop is open for skiing again, while the resort still remains in a state of decay.

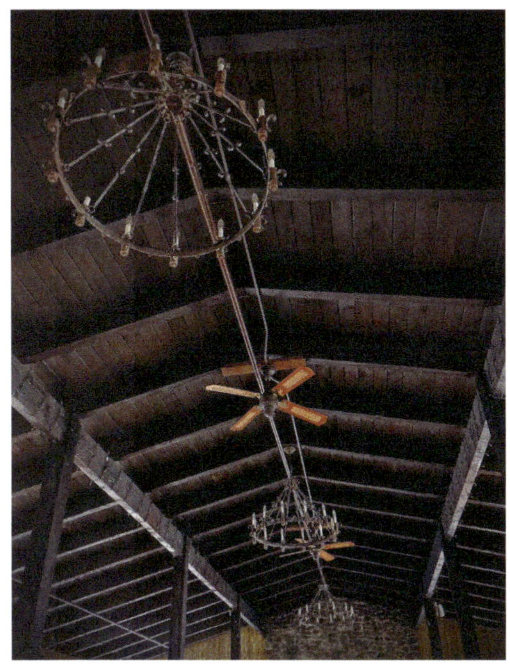

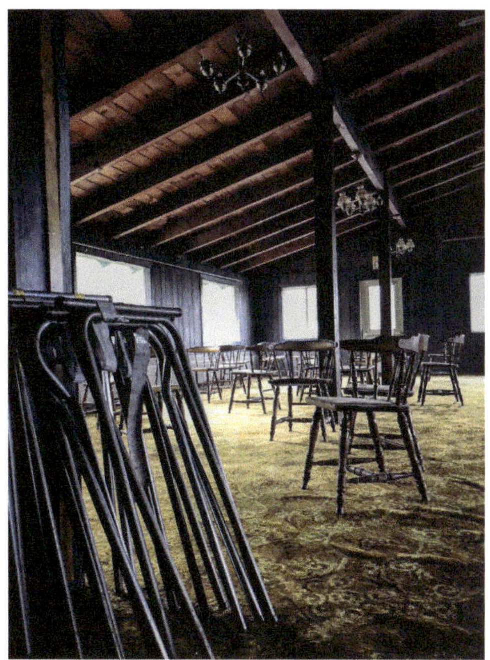

Above left: The old chandeliers and fans with blades made of wood and cane were left hanging in the lodge.

Above right: The piano to the left, not pictured, provided bouts of entertainment, while guests were served using the trays shown here.

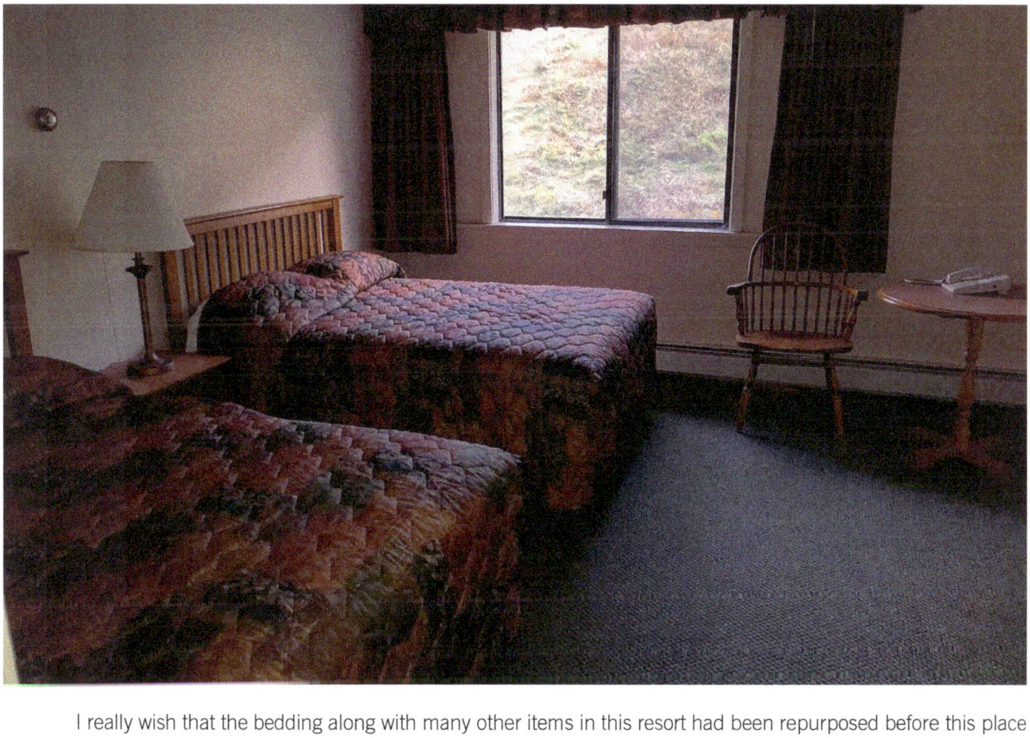

I really wish that the bedding along with many other items in this resort had been repurposed before this place became encompassed in mold.

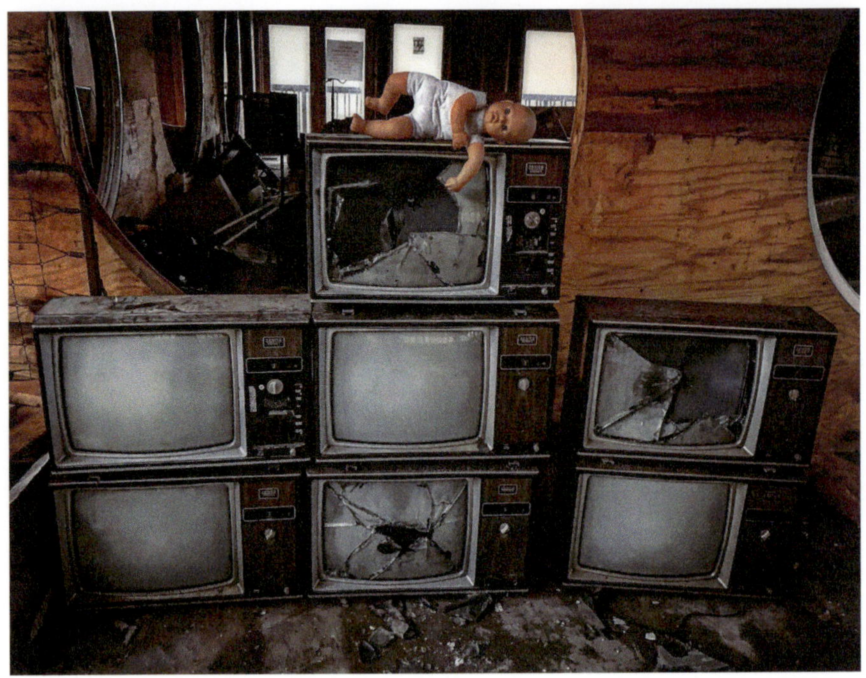

I genuinely wonder how long some little girl has been looking for her baby doll. The smashed TVs exude a sense of creepiness comparable to a horror movie.

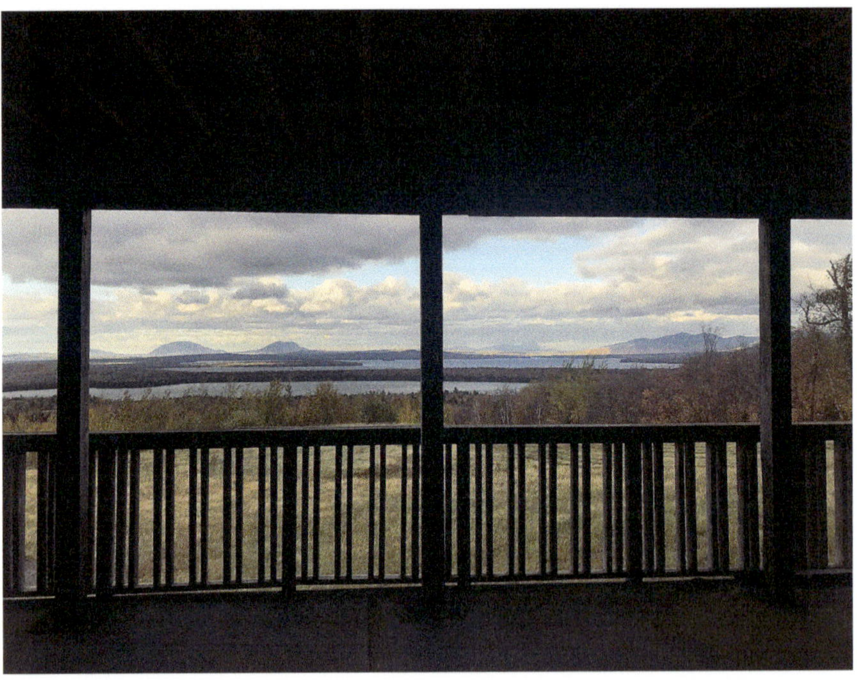

From the summit of the formerly named Big Squaw Mountain, you can see more mountains to the left, overlooking Moosehead Lake.

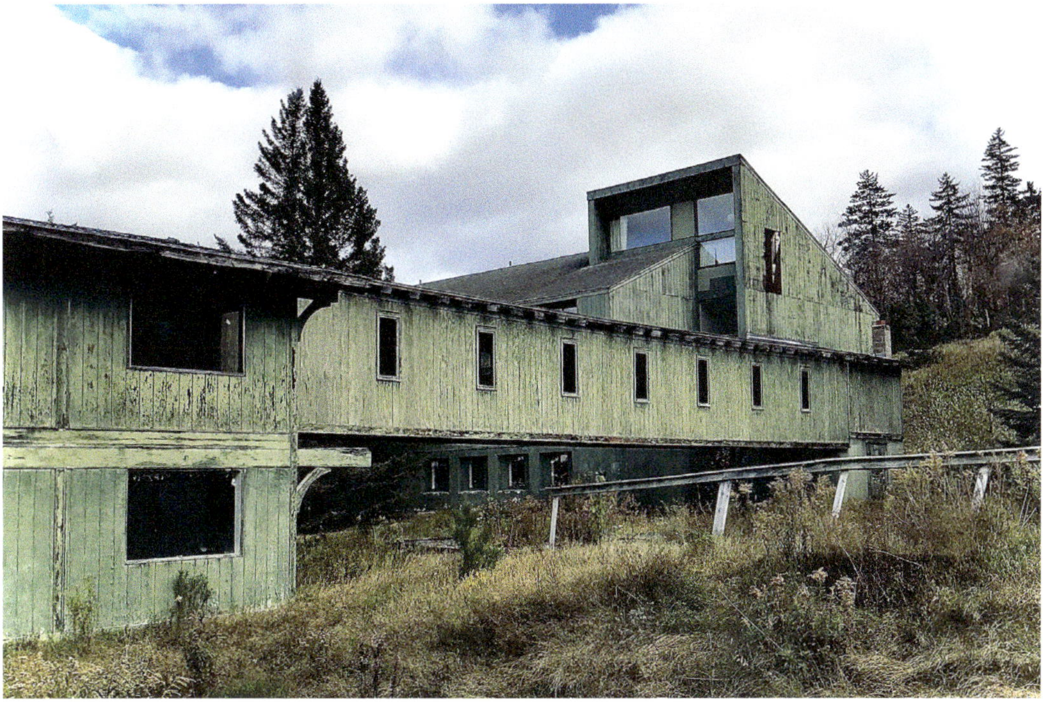

This is a view from the backside of the ski resort.

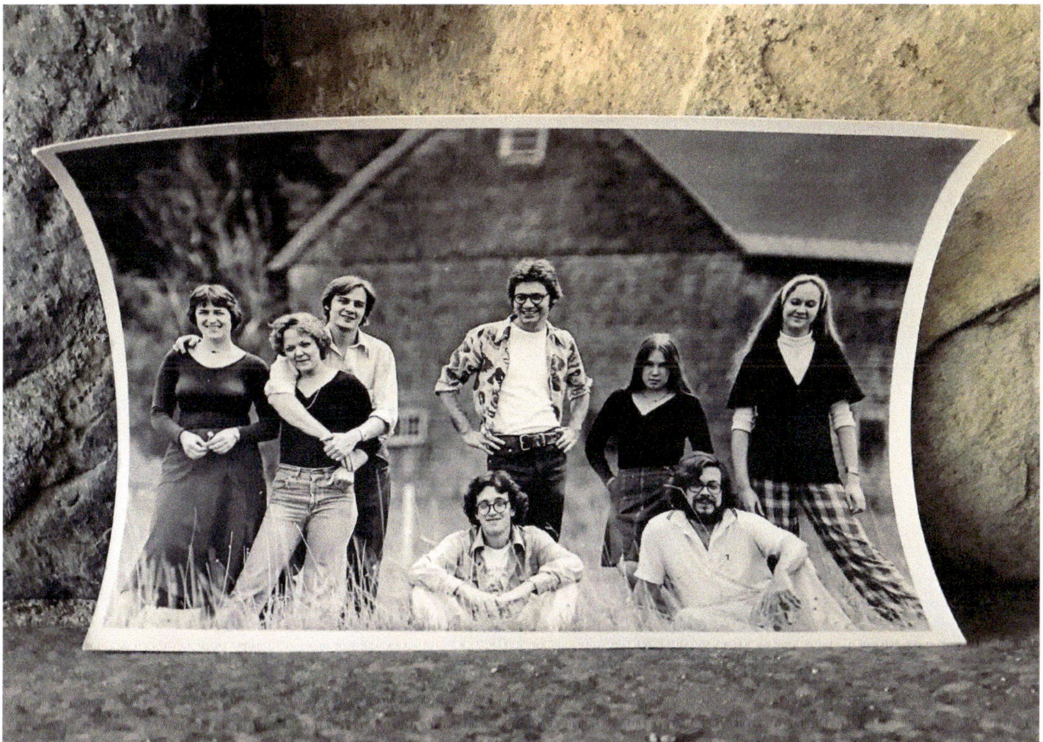

A timeless photograph left behind showcases the fashion trends of that era.

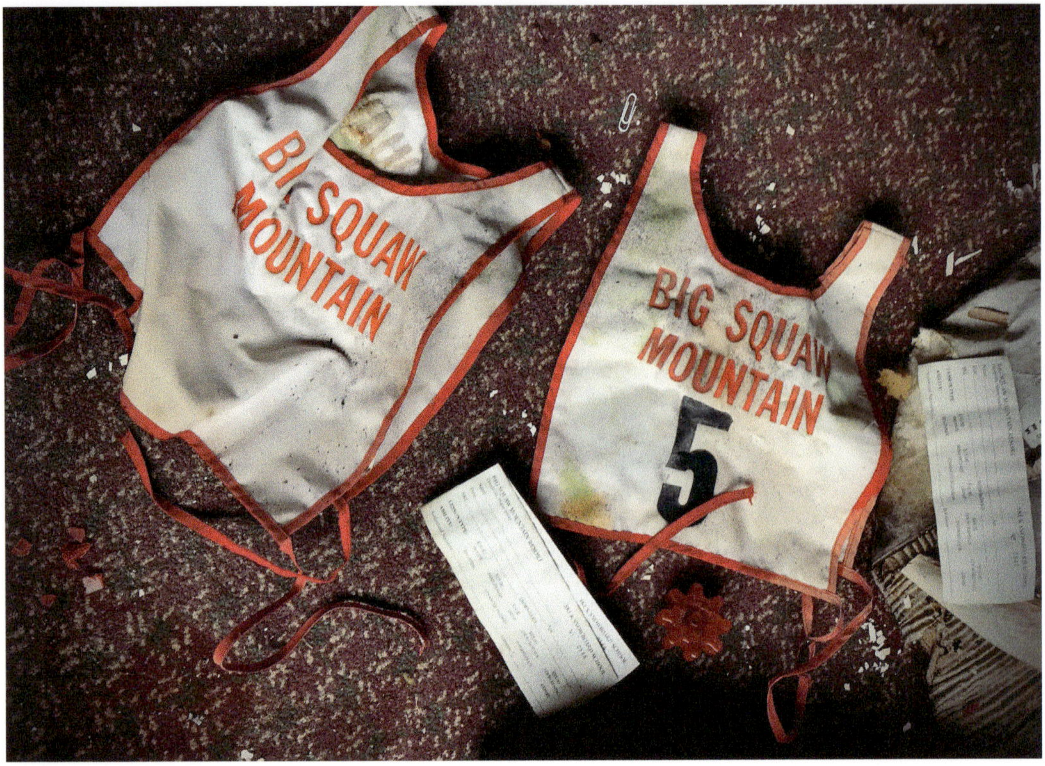

Remnants of a ski team at Big Squaw were revealed by leftover ski bibs strewn across the resort's grimy floor.

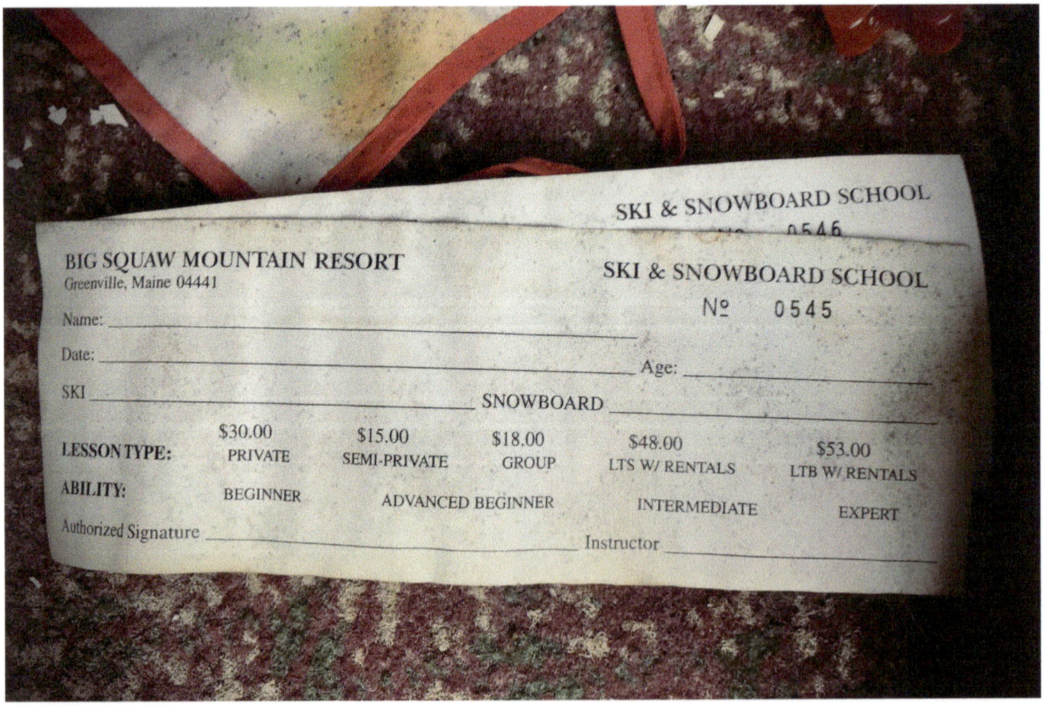

Before technology seemingly took over, these paper slips were utilized at the resort.

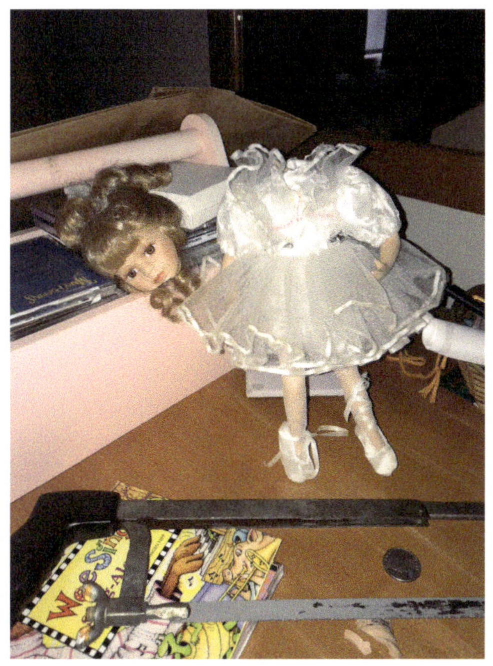

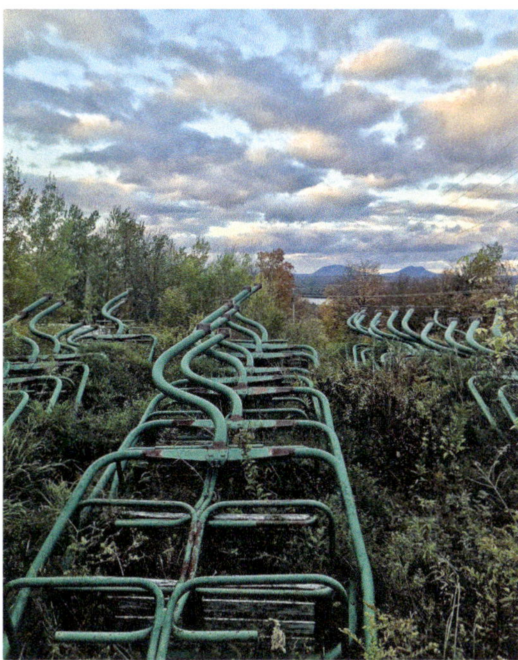

Above left: I'll leave it to your imagination to speculate what occurred here. Your guess is as good as mine. This certainly contributed to the overall spookiness that lingered in the halls.

Above right: The old ski lift chairs sit, deteriorating, never to be used ever again.

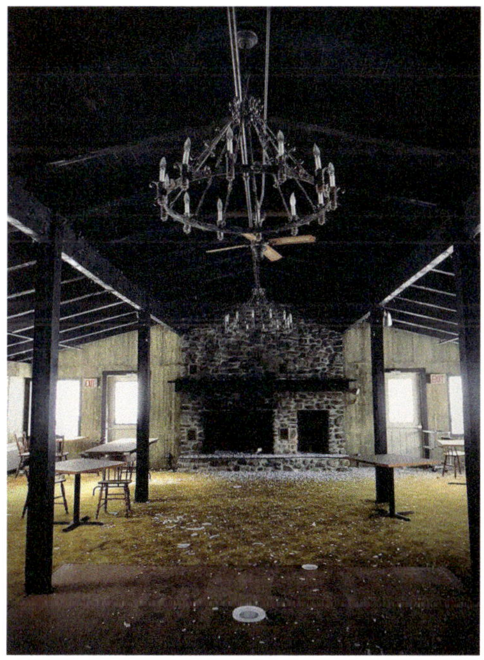

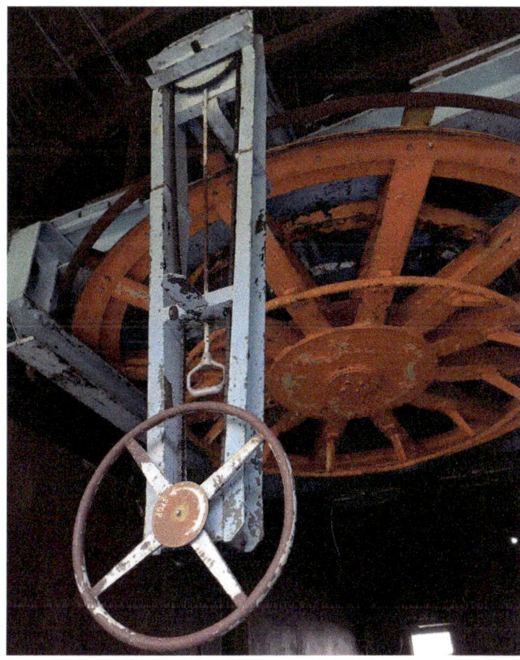

Above left: The lodge exuded vibes reminiscent of a scene from the movie *Dirty Dancing*.

Above right: The bull wheel remains idle at the mountain's summit, adjacent to the control room.

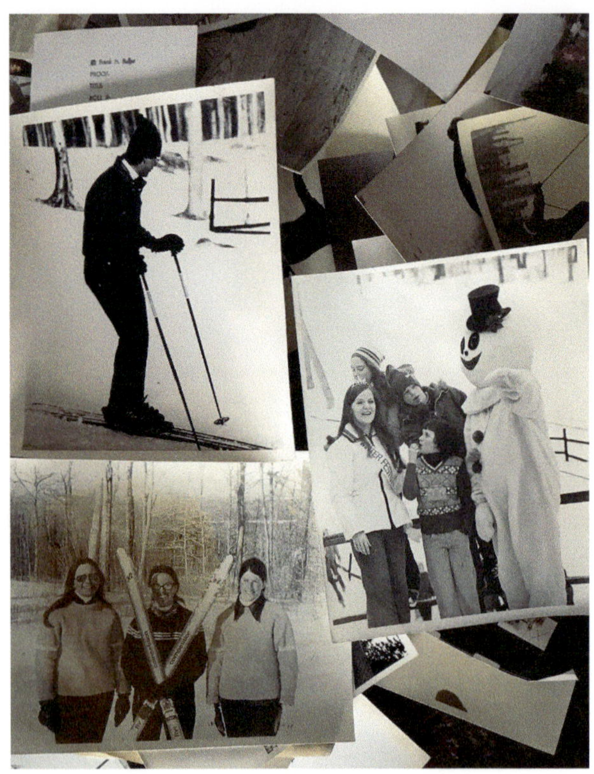

It was quite a pleasant surprise to come across these vintage photographs left behind in the lodge. The young woman pictured with the snowman is adorned with a crown and a sash that reads, "Winter Festival."

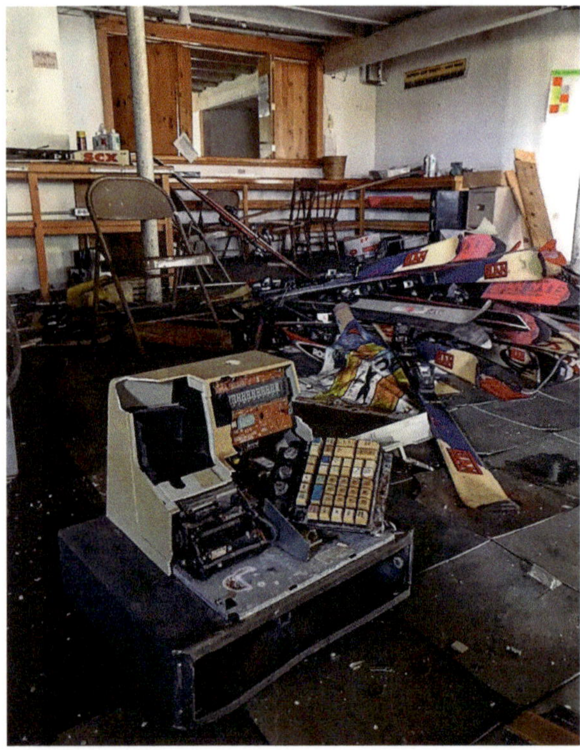

As I glanced around, the haphazardly scattered equipment caught my eye. The sight of a familiar cash register stirred memories of my youth, working alongside my mother in her quilt business, Crystal Creations, which she named after me.

6

MERRILL MEMORIAL MANOR

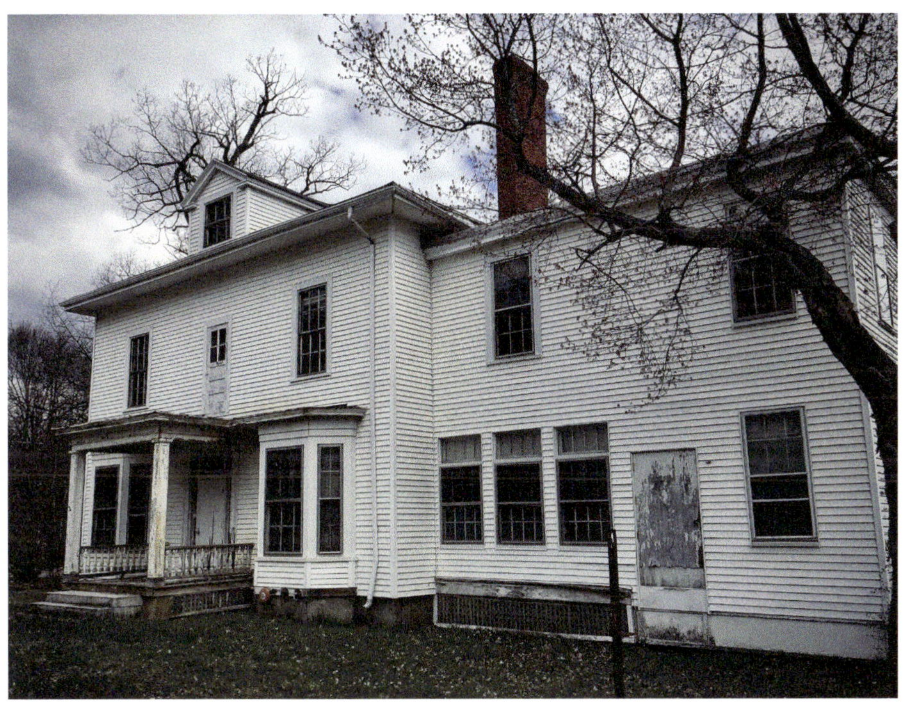

Merrill Memorial Manor, which was a sixty-bed nursing home by the 1970s, had many specialty services available for their patients.

In the tumultuous year of 2020, amid global uncertainty, I seized the opportunity of low gas prices to embark on explorations. During the summer, accompanied by a new friend, Miranda and I ventured into Merrill Memorial Manor. Situated on a quiet road, with two abandoned medical facilities nearby, the manor exuded a haunting aura. While my first solo visit had left me cautious, exploring the entirety of the building felt more secure with a companion by my side. When I was there alone rain seeped through the deteriorating ceiling, casting a melancholic veil over the nurses' station. I made sure to tread carefully, mindful of the decaying floors.

Despite the somber atmosphere, Merrill Memorial Manor held a peculiar charm for me. Drawing on my decade-long experience as a Certified Nursing Assistant, I could envision the inner workings of this former nursing home. Trying to imagine the level of care that once filled the rooms, I navigated through the decaying structure, reminiscing about my own time in similar healthcare settings.

Miranda, a member of a paranormal group, proposed a paranormal investigation at the manor, to which I agreed, intrigued by the opportunity. Armed with a respectful intent and a clear communication approach, we ascended to the third floor, where a meeting room with chairs arranged in a circle awaited us. As we switched off our phones, a paranormal meter lit up, signaling the presence of unseen entities. The gradual illumination of the meter indicated potential ghostly activity, prompting a sense of wonder and excitement within us.

In the midst of our investigation, we both heard distinct footsteps behind us, despite no visible presence besides ourselves. The eerie sensation of a third entity walking alongside us stunned yet excited me, affirming the supernatural energy lingering in the manor. Such unexpected encounters heightened my awareness and curiosity, underscoring the mystique of this place.

Descending to the basement, Miranda initiated a communication attempt with the unseen spirits, seeking clarity and connection. Despite their elusive nature, we received responses through her sound box, including a clear directive to "Get out!" Respecting the ghostly message, we concluded our exploration, acknowledging the boundary between the living and the spiritual realm. Did we spook them or were they saving us from something? The experience left an indelible mark on me, prompting reflection on the unseen forces that coexist at Merrill Memorial Manor.

After our time here, I discovered information about a mass grave containing residents from this manor and two other locations. This revelation sheds light on the intense ghostly energy in the area. The realization that people may unknowingly be walking on a field that serves as a mass grave adds an evocative layer to the atmosphere. The hope for a project to address this sensitive issue where the area can be fenced off with a sign reflects my desire for closure and dignity for the individuals interred in the mass grave.

Interesting Facts about Merrill Memorial Manor

- This Manor was named after Milton Merrill, the original founder of the Merrill Convalescent Home on Brunswick Ave. Milton was the President of the Maine Nursing Homes Association. His wife was a private duty nurse.
- Milton's daughter, Geraldine, received her RN at Greenwood College in Massachusetts. She then acquired the manor with her husband at the current location in 1964 after her father's death, where she became the Director of Nursing.
- Geraldine was known as Mrs. Rankins or Mrs. Wayne Rankins, as that's who she was married to. Her husband, Wayne Rankins, was also the Administrator.
- A new addition was added to the already thirty-bed facility, now known as the extended care facility. On March 15, 1970, an open house was hosted, featuring another thirty beds in the new addition. Rooms were semiprivate and offered individual heat control and adjacent bathrooms.
- Skehan's Diary provided the manor with dairy products and fresh vegetables.
- Augusta Supply Co. supplied the new addition with their electrical services.
- Mutual Lumber dispensed the building materials.
- Special services for patients included an Advisory Physician, Dental Consultant, Religious Advisor, Pharmaceutical Consultant, Professional Dietitian, Social Services Consultant, Physical Therapy Consultant, Speech Therapy Consultant, and Occupational Therapy Consultant.
- By 1970, Donna Holmes, RN, was the Supervisor of Nurses, and Bruce Alexander was the Assoc. Administrator.
- The main purpose of this manor was to provide restorative services for patients who no longer needed regular hospital facilities, but needed follow up care.

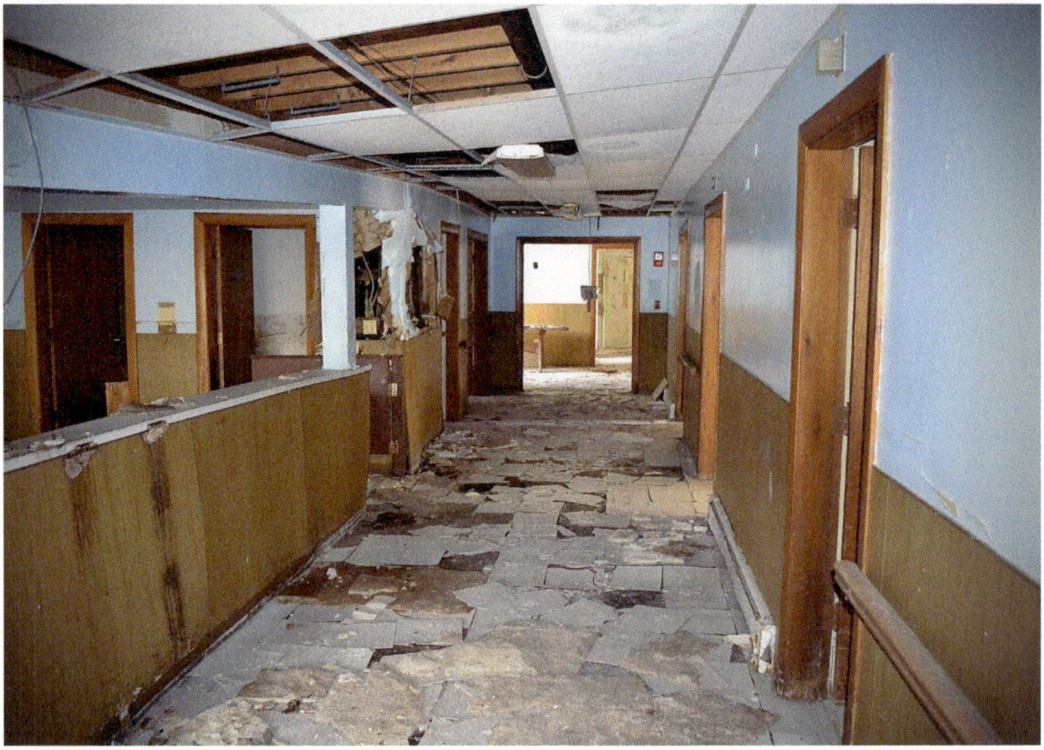

The room numbers are still displayed on the doors. To the left, a nurse's station is in immediate danger of falling through the deteriorating floor.

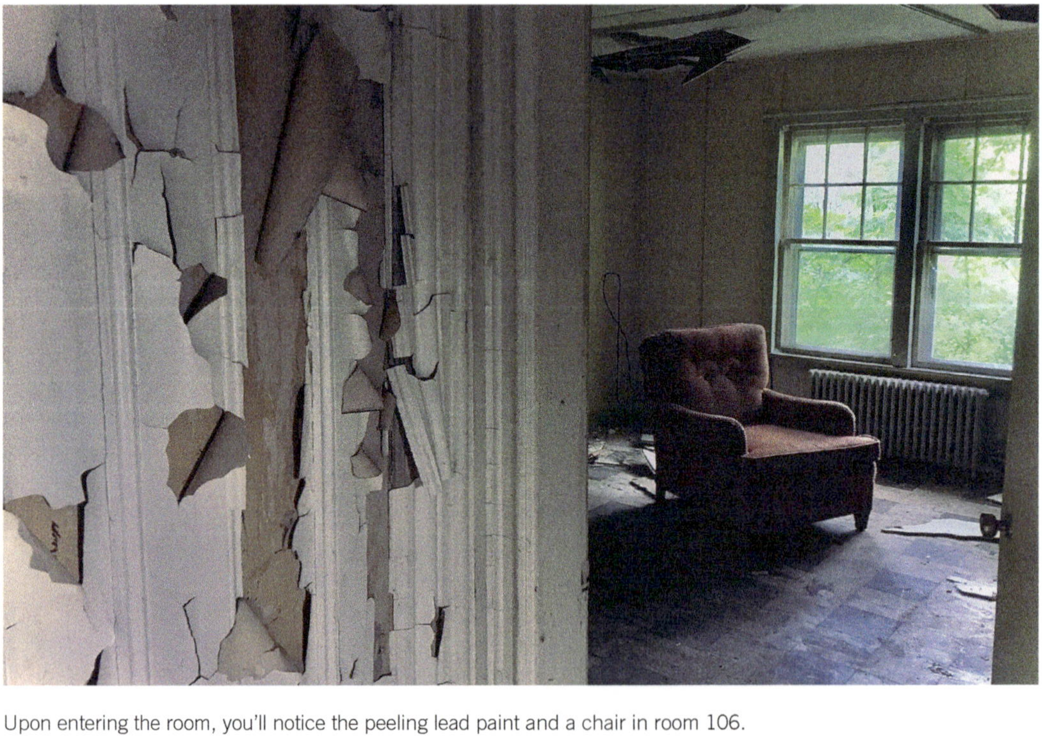

Upon entering the room, you'll notice the peeling lead paint and a chair in room 106.

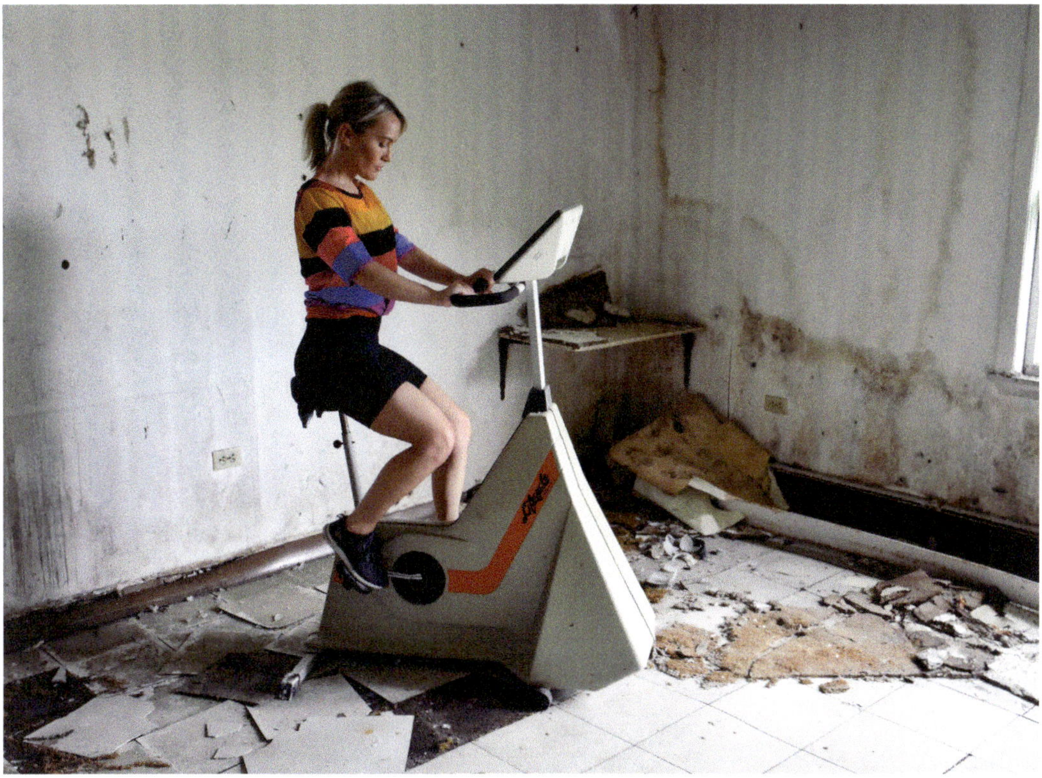

Here, my stunning friend Miranda poses for a picture on the exercise bike.

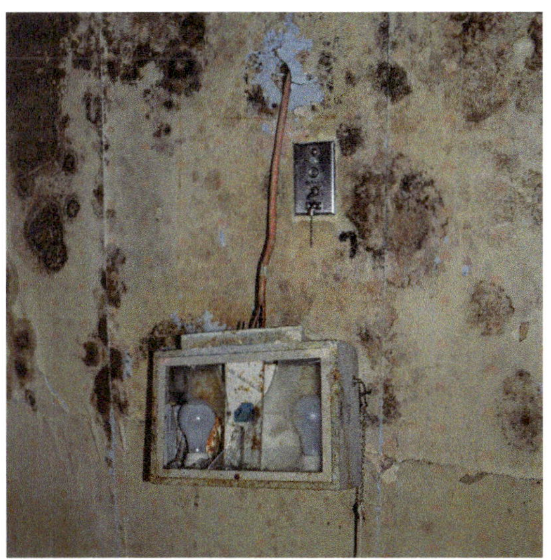

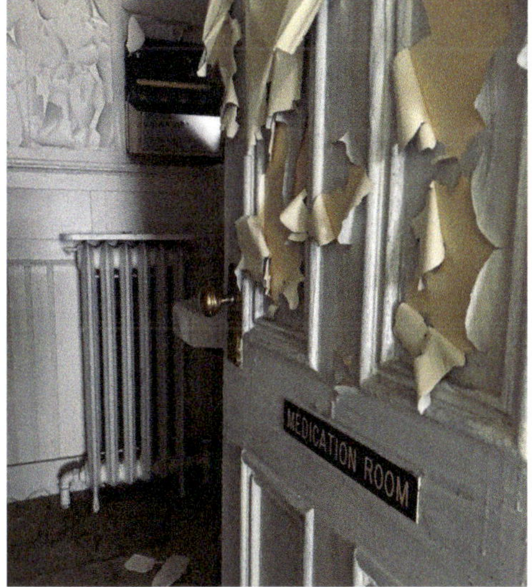

Above left: This call bell system was used by residents to request assistance, but modern methods have rendered the need for light bulbs obsolete.

Above right: Medication rooms were commonly used before the introduction of medication carts in nursing homes. They were typically located in a central area of the facility and were staffed by nurses or medication aides who were responsible for managing and dispensing medications to residents.

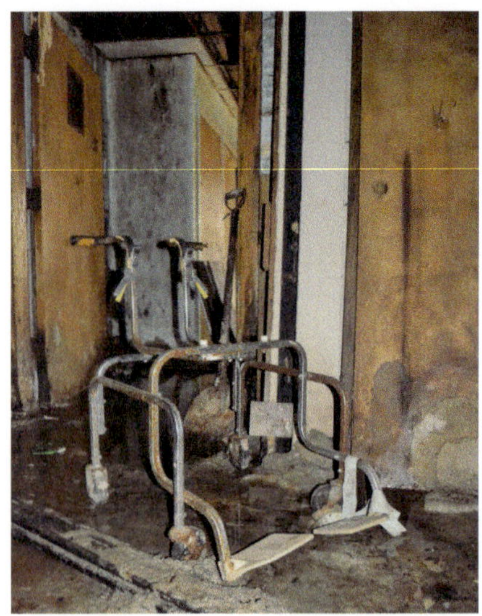

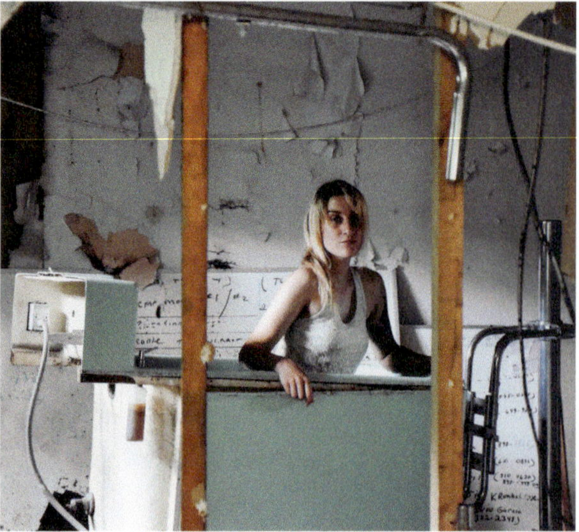

Above left: Remnants of an old wheelchair sits in the basement, unaware of its impending fate as it waits for the nurses' station above to collapse on top of it.

Above right: I remember starting my first CNA job at a nursing home in 2008 at the age of seventeen, where I assisted residents with whirlpool baths in these specific types of tubs. It was my turn to pose for a picture. [*Miranda Dolph*]

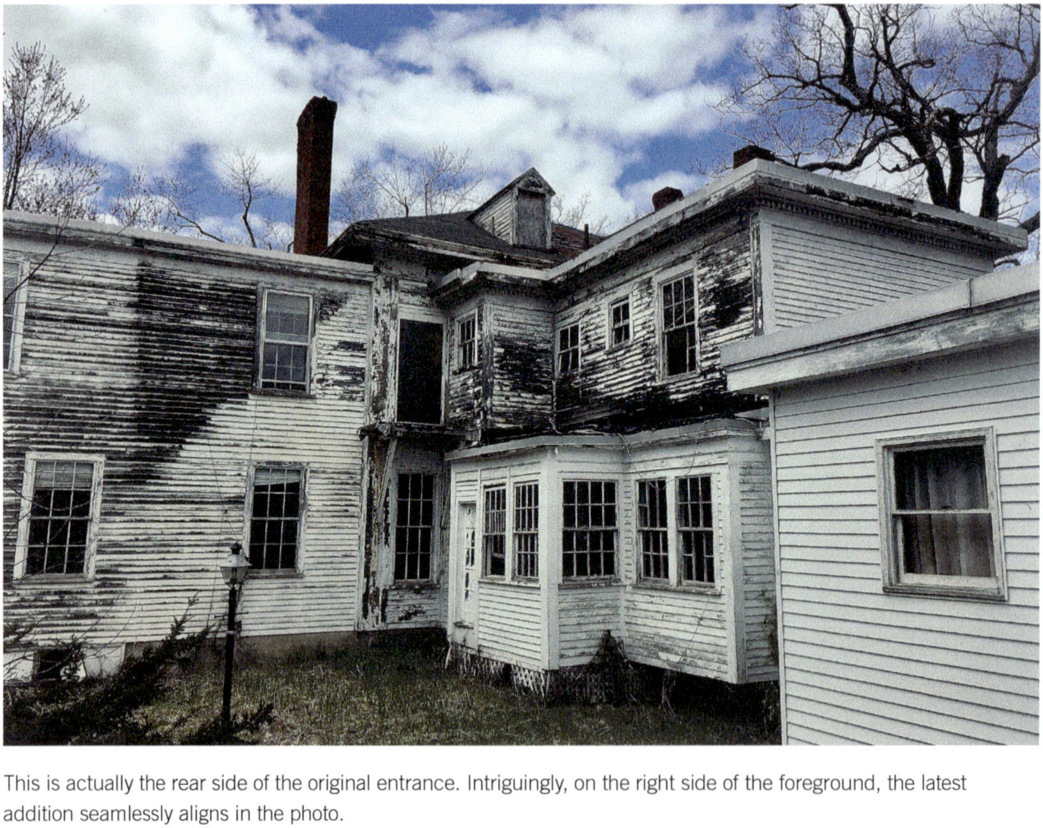

This is actually the rear side of the original entrance. Intriguingly, on the right side of the foreground, the latest addition seamlessly aligns in the photo.

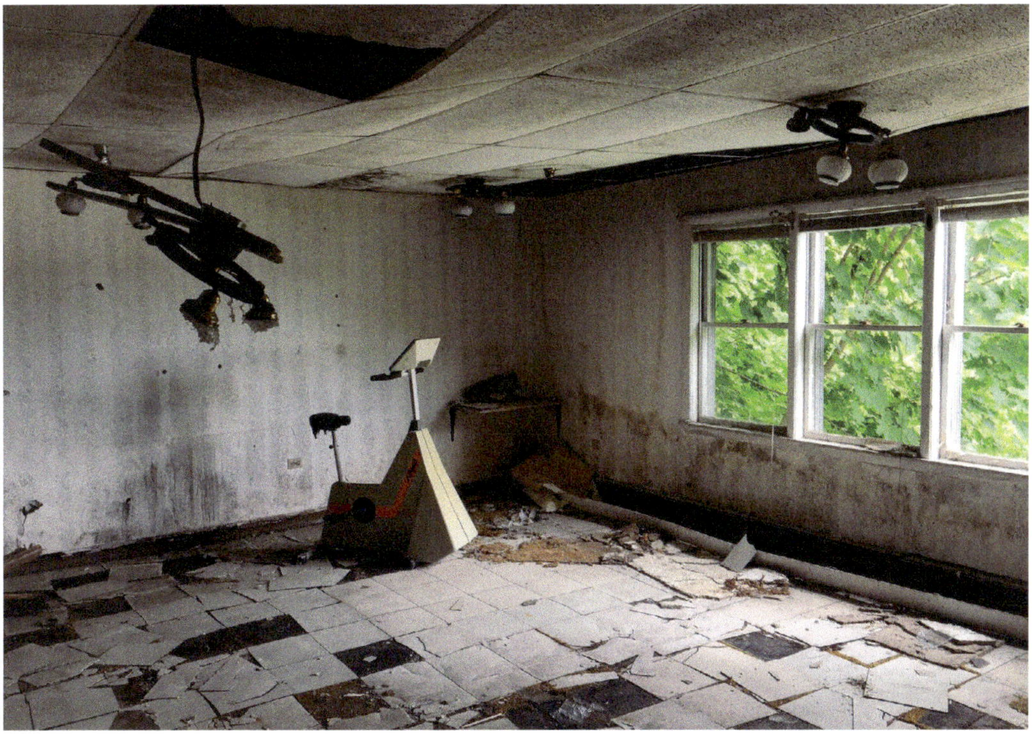

Next to the nurses' station, this open room is where various patients would gather to enjoy their meals and listen to the soothing melodies of the piano.

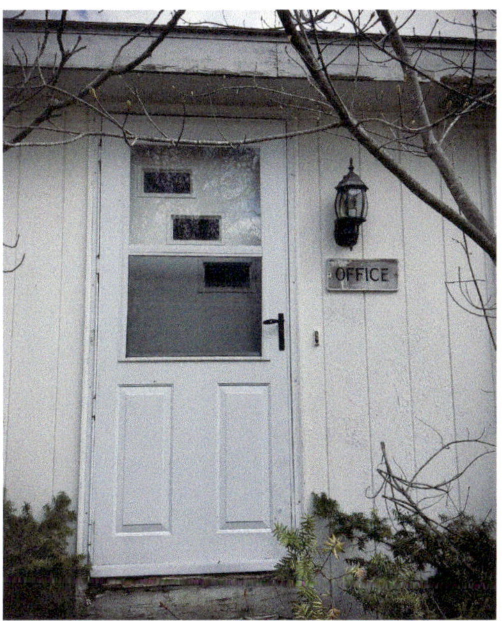

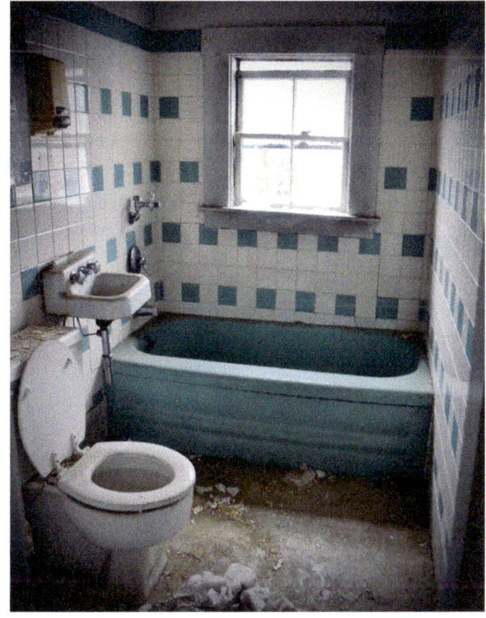

Above left: In 1970, a second entrance was constructed after the new addition was built. To access it, one had to pass the office before reaching the entrance of the building.

Above right: These tiles were strategically placed to create a stunning pattern in this bathroom.

7

GARDINER GENERAL MEMORIAL HOSPITAL

In 1918, this hospital was opened in Central Maine, coincidentally during the pandemic of the Spanish Flu, also known as Influenza. During its first year, the hospital was taxed significantly due to the number of influenza patients that it admitted. To handle the overwhelming number of admissions, the nursing staff received support from both employees and community volunteers. Led by Houlton native Violet E. Robinson, the team effectively managed the situation and provided care to the large volume of patients affected.

It was devastating news when Miss Robinson succumbed to the illness and passed away. To address the crisis of the pandemic, the Maine Red Cross urgently appealed for volunteers, irrespective of their nursing background, to lend a hand in caring for the sick. The response was incredible, with nursing students from Augusta General Hospital traveling to Bath to provide assistance, tragically resulting in some of them losing their lives. As the demand for medical aid escalated, newspapers carried advertisements seeking nurses, and the pleas in local community columns took on a tone of heightened urgency.

During that period, people affected by influenza had scarce alternatives beyond hospital treatment. In a time without antibiotics, the options for medical intervention were limited. Doctors could only suggest conventional influenza remedies such as rest, hydration, fresh air, and aspirin. Within certain households, families turned to traditional remedies like onion poultices and mustard plasters.

In Maine, newspapers were brimming with advertisements for patent medicines, all promising a cure for influenza. Vicks "Vaporub" rose to fame during the 1918 pandemic. The proliferation of advertisements for over-the-counter commercial medicines was evident during this time.

The *Bangor Daily News* published this recipe for others to learn and utilize for themselves on October 19, 1819. I've included it here, word for word, to ensure it doesn't get lost to time and to serve as a reminder that there are alternative methods to heal our bodies beyond solely relying on Western Medicine. As a nurse's aide of ten years working in a variety of settings and living through the COVID-19 pandemic, I can sincerely empathize with what they went through.

Grandma's Poultice

Take 6-8 onions, chop fine, put in a large spider over a hot fire, then add about the same amount of rye meal and vinegar - enough to form a thick paste. Let mixture simmer 5-10 minutes, stirring occasionally. Put in a cotton bag large enough to cover the lungs and apply to the chest as hot as the patient can bear it. Continue till perspiration starts freely from the chest.

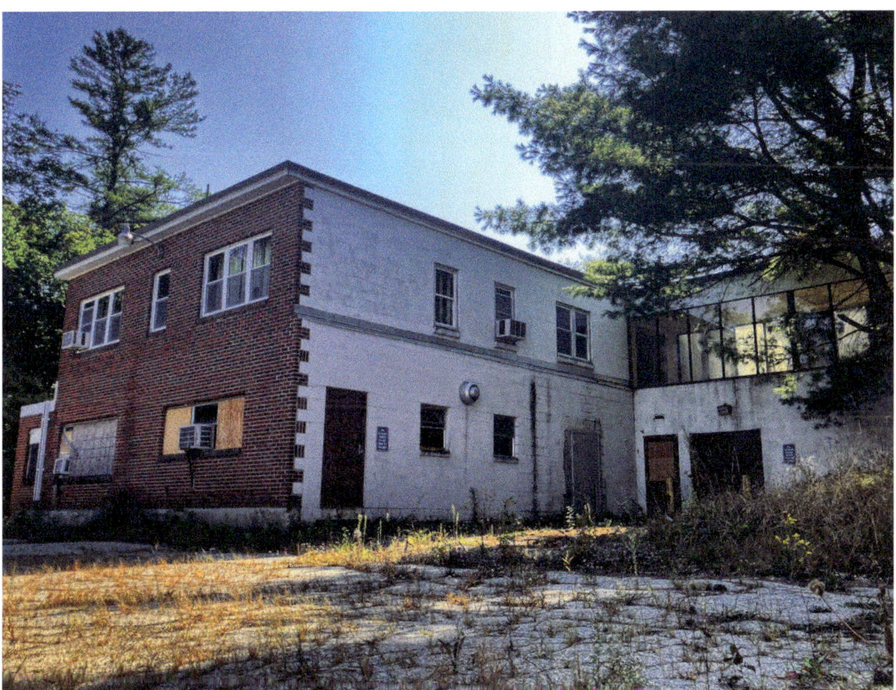

This was the first hospital in Maine that I got to explore.

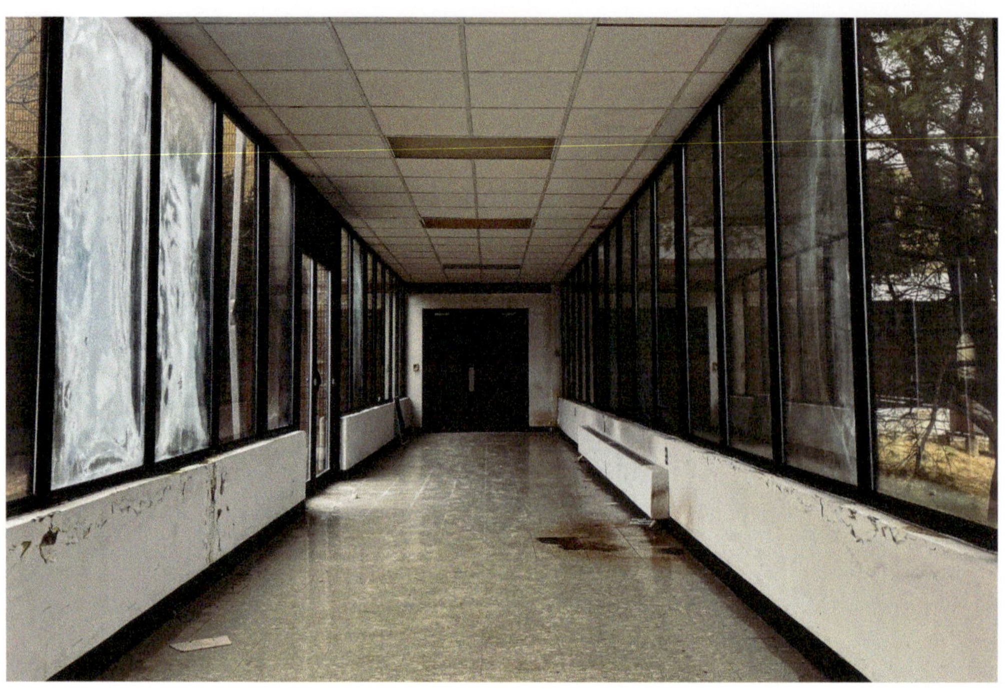

The corridor was silent, with only ghosts drifting by for company.

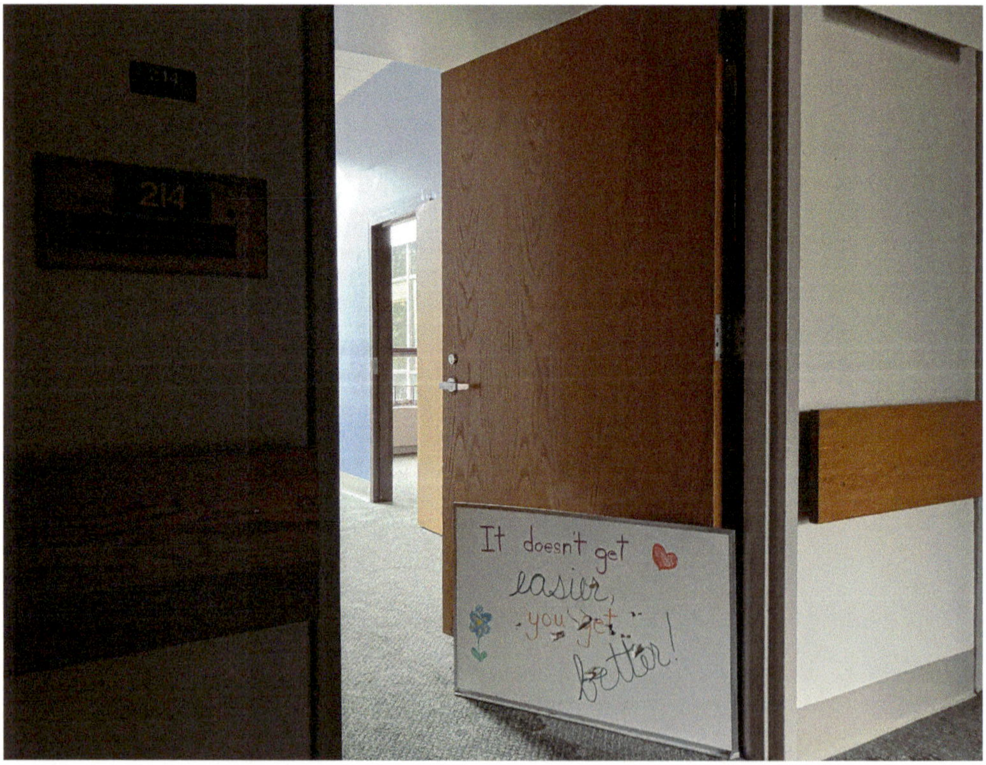

“It doesn’t get easier; you get better!” A heartfelt message, likely written to a patient, by one of the nurses.

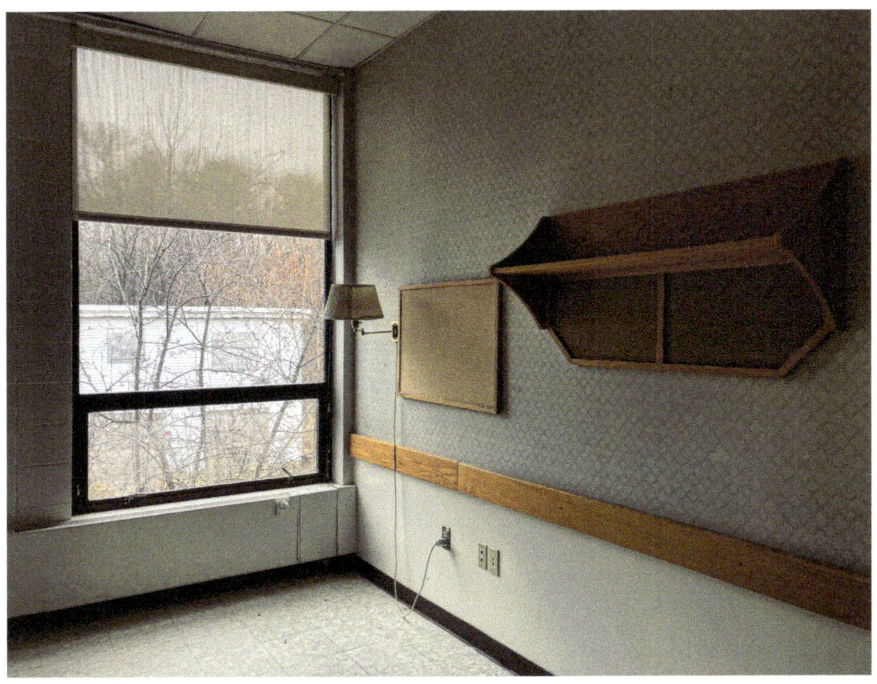

From this hospital room, Merrill Memorial Manor was visible. I pondered about how many patients had looked out the window, only to realize their fate lay across the street.

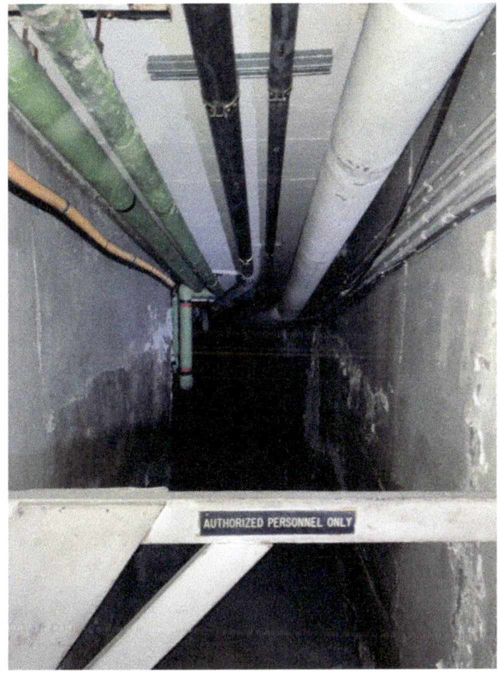

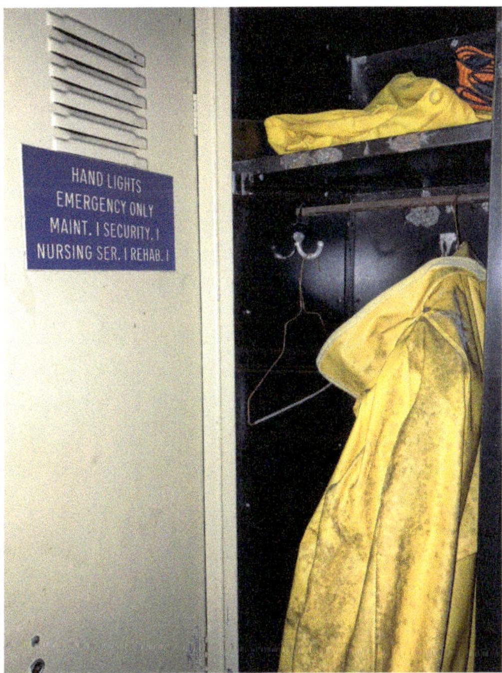

Above left: Upon our initial arrival, my friend and I traversed a lengthy underground tunnel that led to a maintenance room, eventually opening up to a garage.

Above right: Lockers were stocked with supplies, as if someone were planning to return.

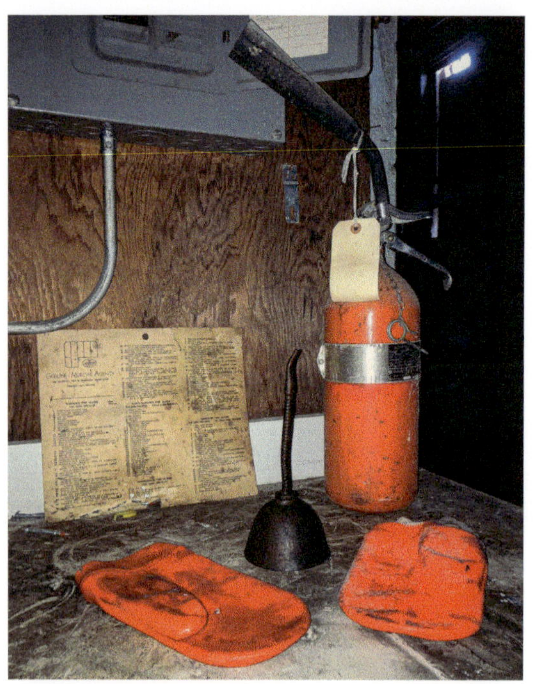

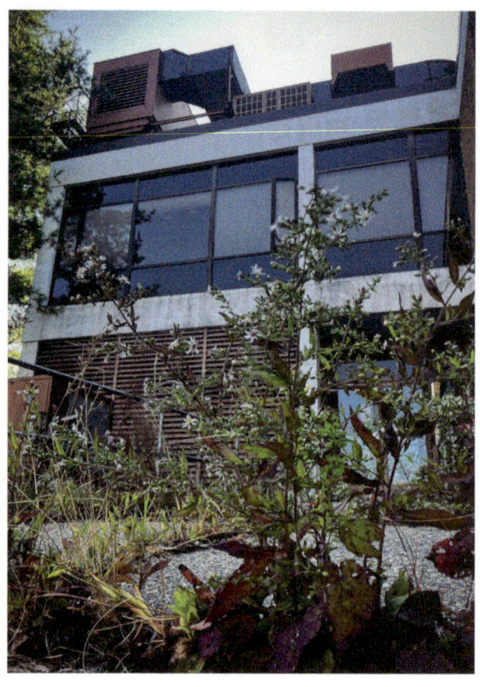

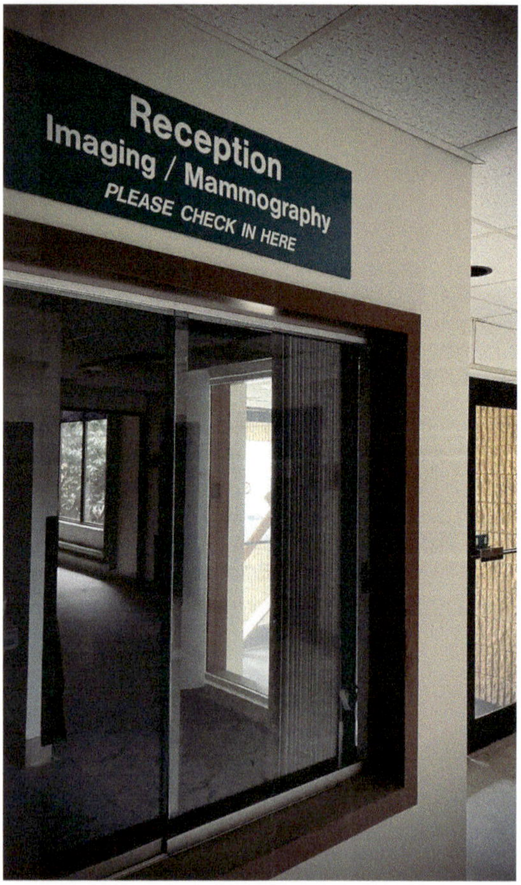

Above left: In this image, a classic thumb pump oiler is featured among other miscellaneous items found on a workbench.

Above right: This is the back entrance of the hospital.

Left: Patients would arrive at this location to check in for imaging services.

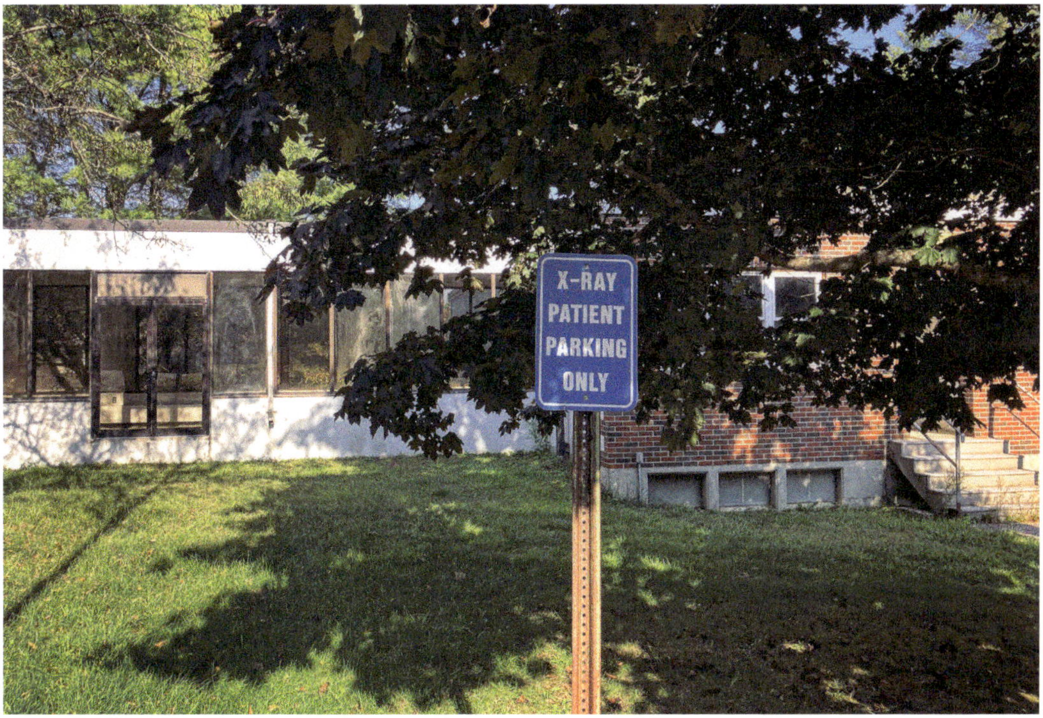

I thought it was neat how these signs were still left. I also liked how people who needed x-rays got their own parking spots.

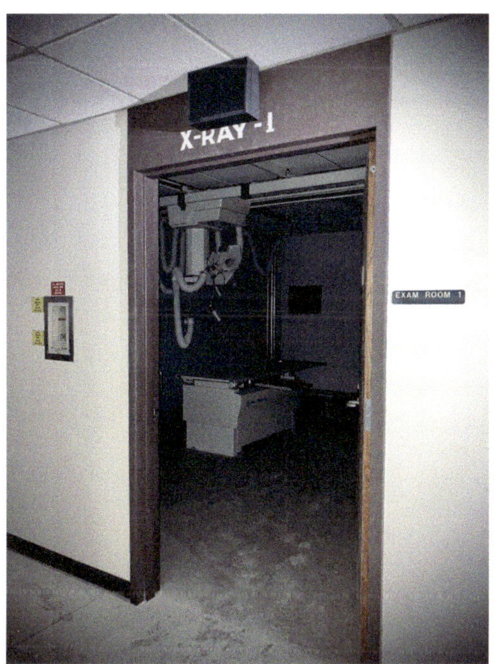

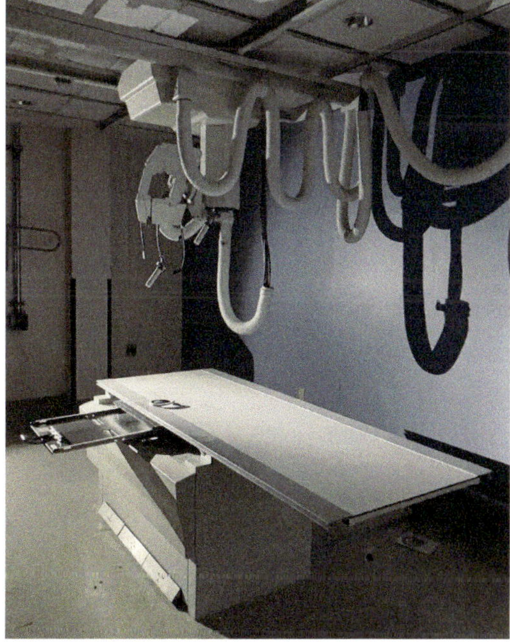

Above left: To my surprise, the x-ray room still housed leftover equipment from the hospital's golden era.

Above right: The medical equipment remained in place, a clear indication that it wasn't easy to dispose of.

8

THE OTIS PAPER MILL

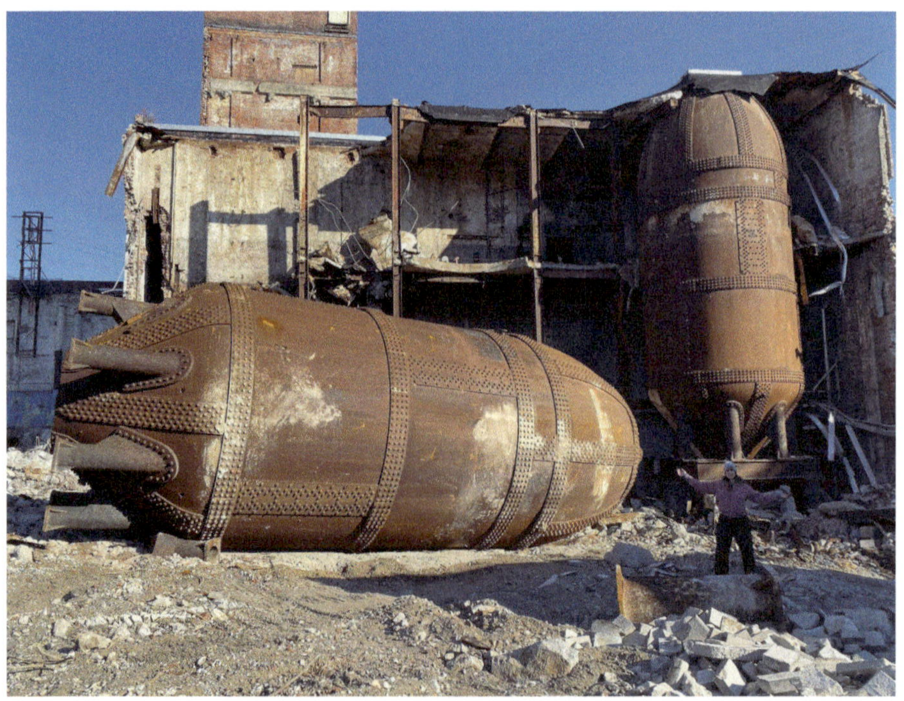

These digester tanks were once used to turn wood chips into pulp, using acid and steam. You can see the size of them in this picture compared to me. [*Moss Man*]

Since its inception, paper has played a momentous role in Maine's economy, influencing the identities of both individuals and communities, and leaving a lasting impact on the environment across the state. In 1888, Hugh Chisholm's establishment of the Otis Falls Pulp Company in Jay marked a significant moment in the history of papermaking in the country. The mill quickly became one of the most advanced facilities of its kind in the nation, linking Maine's paper industry to markets both nationally and globally. Over the following hundred years, Maine solidified its position as a world leader in the production of pulp and paper, shaping the state's economic landscape for generations to come.

Hugh Chisholm's foray into the paper industry commenced with modest origins, as he sold newspapers on trains to fund his college studies. Following his relocation to Portland in 1872, Chisholm's enterprising nature prompted him to delve into the paper sector. According to past stories, in 1882, a frigid winter day found Chisholm in Rumford, riding in a sleigh, where he was captivated by the potential for a business venture upon beholding the awe-inspiring Rumford Falls. Motivated by this striking scene, he embarked on a mission to harness the power of the Androscoggin River, founding paper mills in Jay, Rumford, and Livermore Falls, thereby initiating his enduring impact on Maine's paper industry.

Initially a small operation with just one machine, the mill was officially incorporated as the Otis Falls Pulp & Paper Company in 1888, with Chisholm at its helm as president. The mill experienced rapid growth when Edwin Riley joined the venture in 1894. By 1897, a significant milestone was reached as efforts began to consolidate various small mills in the region. With Chisholm's guidance and the collaboration of a select group, the International Paper Company was established, absorbing more than twenty independent paper and pulp mills. Within that same year, Chisholm assumed the role of president at the International Paper Company, a position he held until 1907. Around this period, the Otis Mill transformed into one of the largest newspaper print mills globally, making its mark on the industry.

Otis

The bricks they are broken,
Like so many of us,
Yet they don't say a word,
They don't make a fuss.

To think this was a livelihood,
Day after day,
To have it all,
Just taken away,

Calendars still hung,
Winterized notes on the door,
Moldy toilet seats,
And a creaky tech floor.

The laboratory empty,
Without humans, not supplies,
Chemicals and test tubes left,
Along with multiple whys.

The pulper sat dormant,
The lead paint chipping away,
It once was a booming papermill,
Back in the day.

An end of an era,
By the river no more,
Otis was its name,
Soon forgotten, I'm sure.

- Crystal Eastman
November 28, 2023

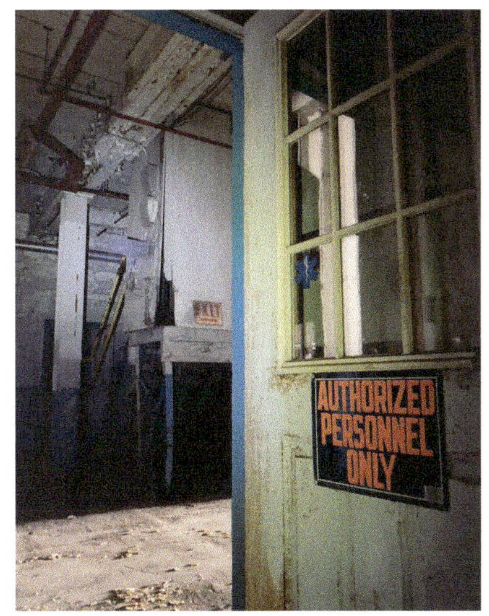

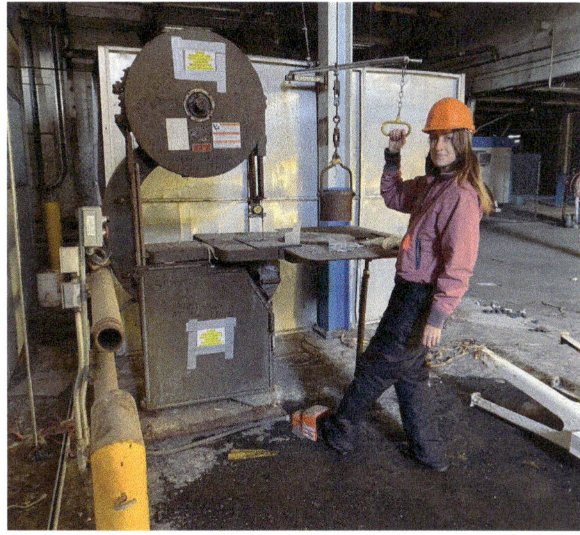

Above left: This unsettling image captures the darkness of the place, where flashlights were crucial for exploration. I can almost feel the coldness of that day when looking at this picture.

Above right: I'm pretending to operate the bandsaw one last time before this place is razed. [*Moss Man*]

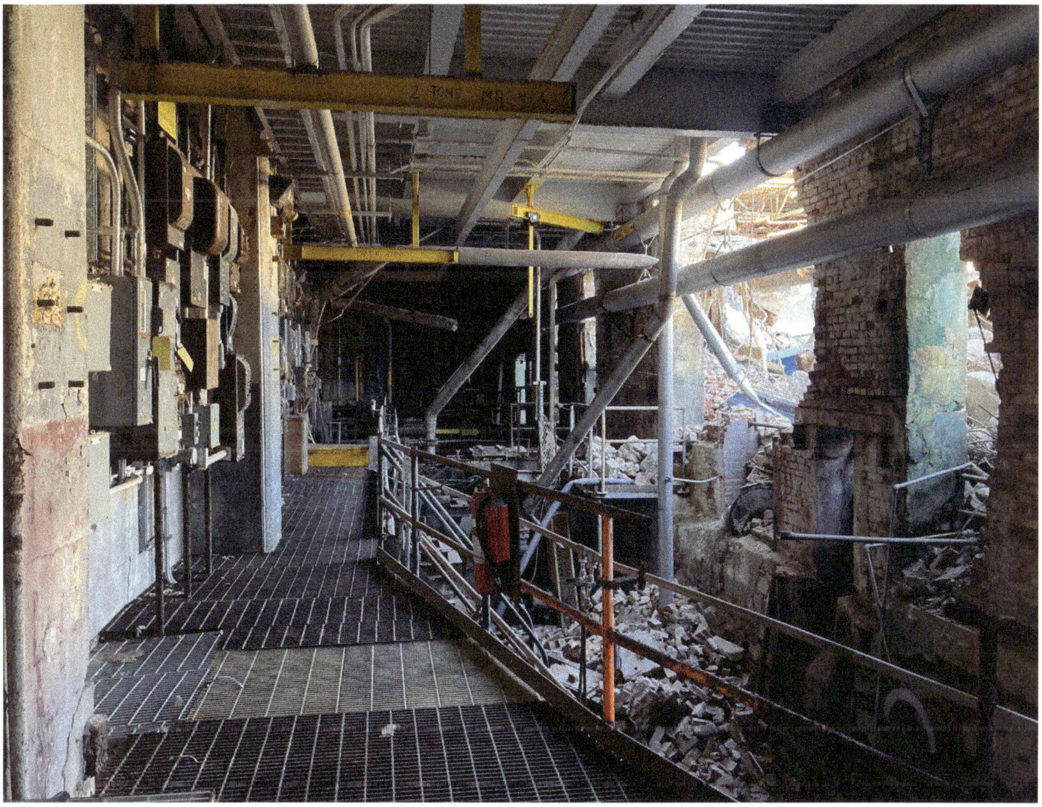

This was the view upon entering the mill. The sheer size of it meant that one could easily get turned around if not paying attention.

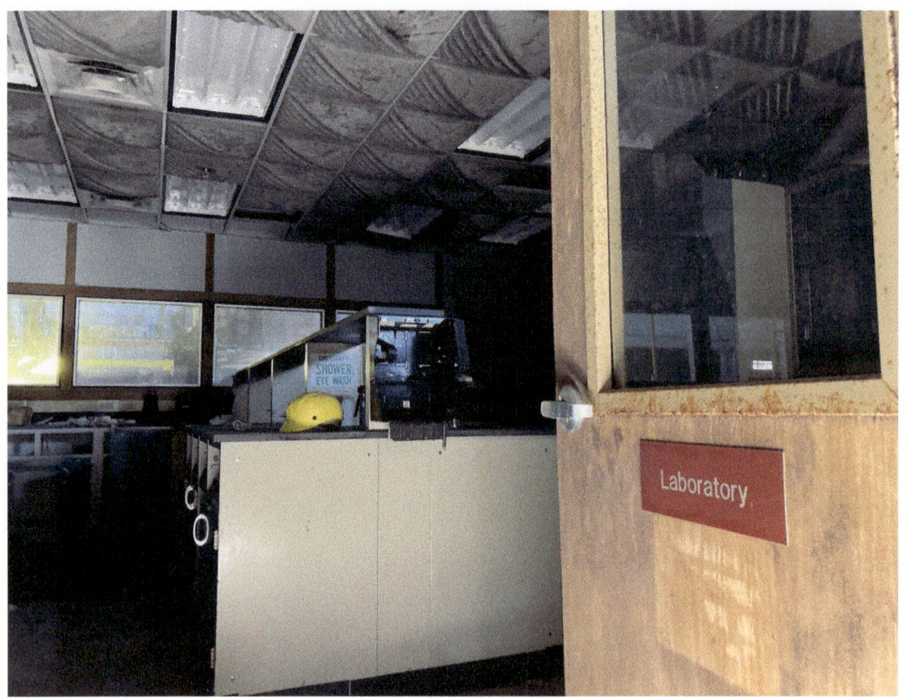

The laboratory was a delightful find for me. It was a component of the tech center that had been incorporated later on.

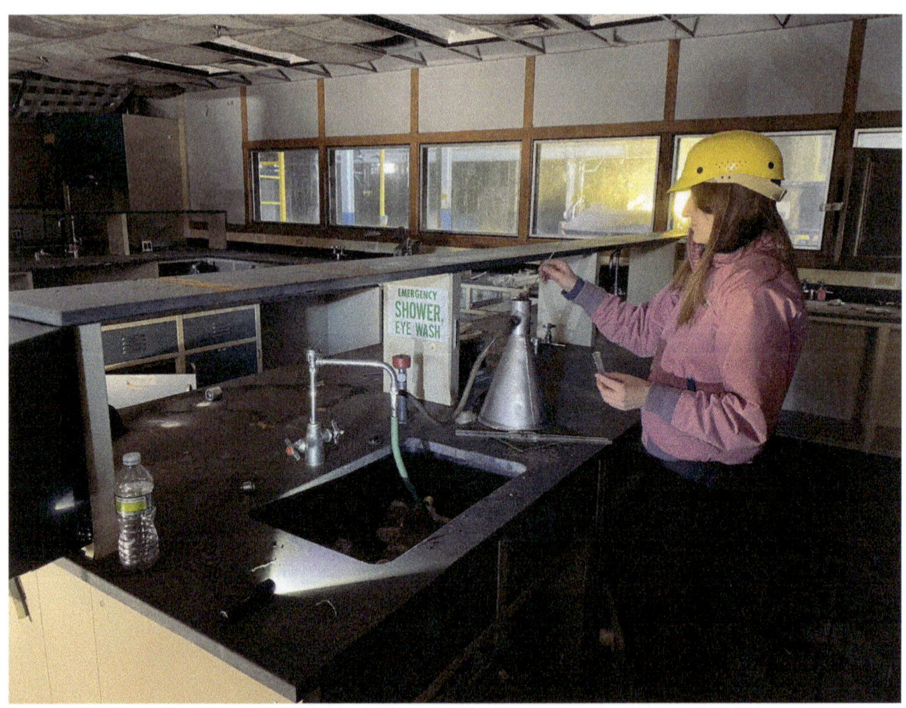

In this picture my friend captured me as I examined some of the old lab equipment. [*Moss Man*]

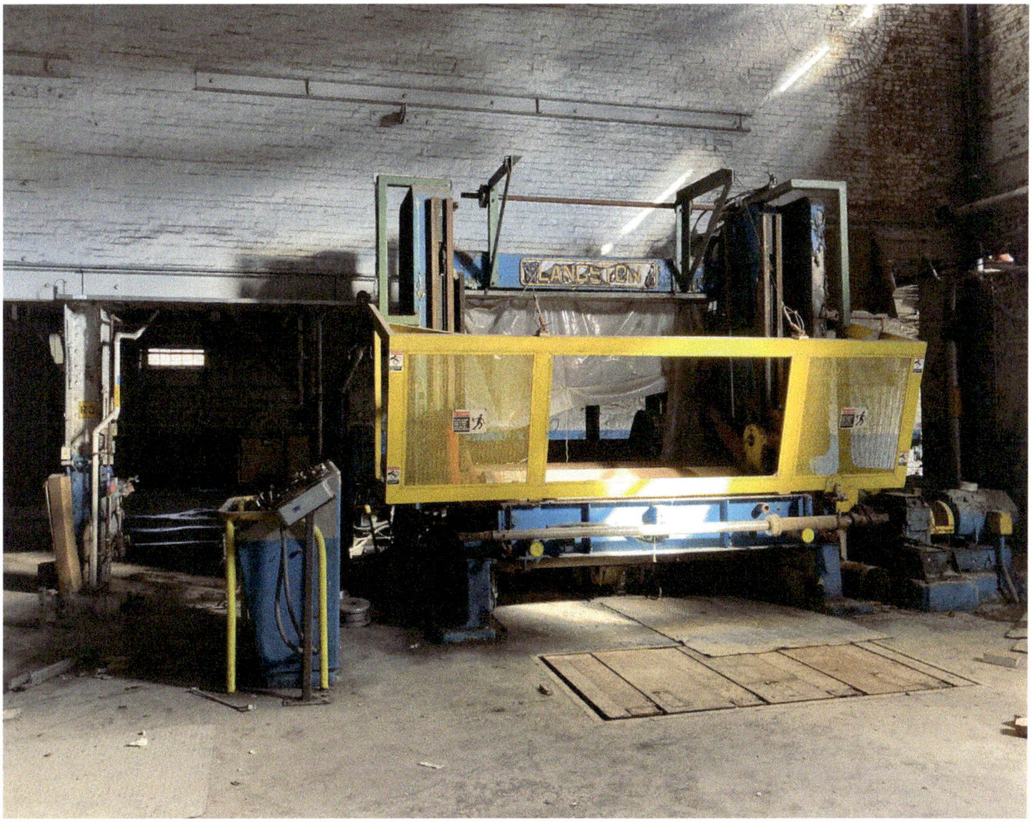

This salvage winder was used for correcting defects in the finished paper rolls.

I was captivated by the fact that they had engraved this onto the wall, preserving a piece of history that commemorated the final day at the paper mill. Explorers like myself are lucky to experience such sights firsthand.

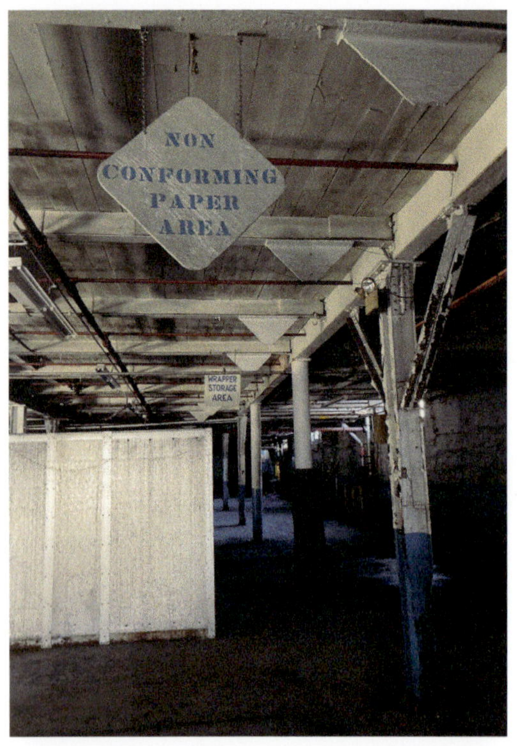

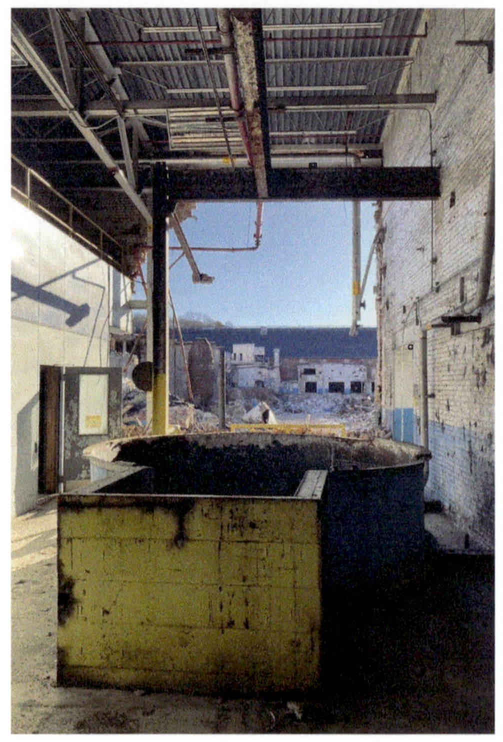

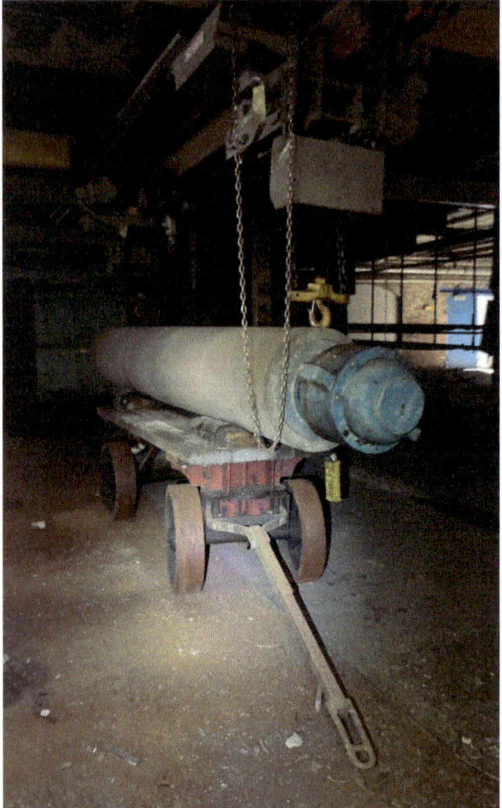

Above left: In this area, they stored paper rolls that didn't pass testing or physical examination.

Above right: This is a twelve-foot pulper. One of my favorite parts about exploring here was that I got the privilege to have a tour by a former employee.

Left: A granite roll that was once used at the wet end of the paper machine, sits left behind.

9

MAINE'S TRAINS

Maine's railroad history is a tapestry woven with innovation, expansion, and the transformative power of locomotion. The state's railroads played a crucial role in shaping its economic landscape, connecting rural communities, facilitating trade, and spurring industrial growth.

The Bangor & Piscataquis Canal & Railroad completed the first line of tracks in 1836, linking Bangor to Old Town. This milestone made it the second railroad in New England, with the Boston & Lowell Railroad having started operations in 1835. Driven by the need to transport goods and people efficiently across the rugged terrain, more rail lines formed quickly. The construction of these lines, often through challenging landscapes, heralded a new era of connectivity and prosperity for the state. The Maine rail system expanded rapidly, linking urban centers like Portland and Bangor with remote towns and villages.

One of the most iconic aspects of Maine's railroad history is the prevalence of steam locomotives, which chugged through the charming countryside, billowing smoke and steam as they traversed the tracks. These iron giants were the workhorses of the railroads, hauling timber, agricultural products, and passengers across the state with efficiency and power. As railroads flourished in Maine, so did the ingenuity of those involved in the industry. From the construction of roundhouses and turntables for locomotive maintenance and storage to the development of new rail technology, Maine's railroad engineers and workers have left their mark on the state's history.

Over the years, Maine's railroads witnessed significant transformations, with the rise of diesel locomotives, streamlined passenger trains, and the eventual decline of passenger rail service in certain areas. Today, Maine's railroads continue to play a vital role in the state's transportation infrastructure, carrying freight, supporting local industries, and offering scenic rail excursions for tourists and history enthusiasts. In addition, there is a Swedish Boxcar that has been transformed into a unique bookstore. Several locations in Maine also offer rail cycling, both for visitors to enjoy.

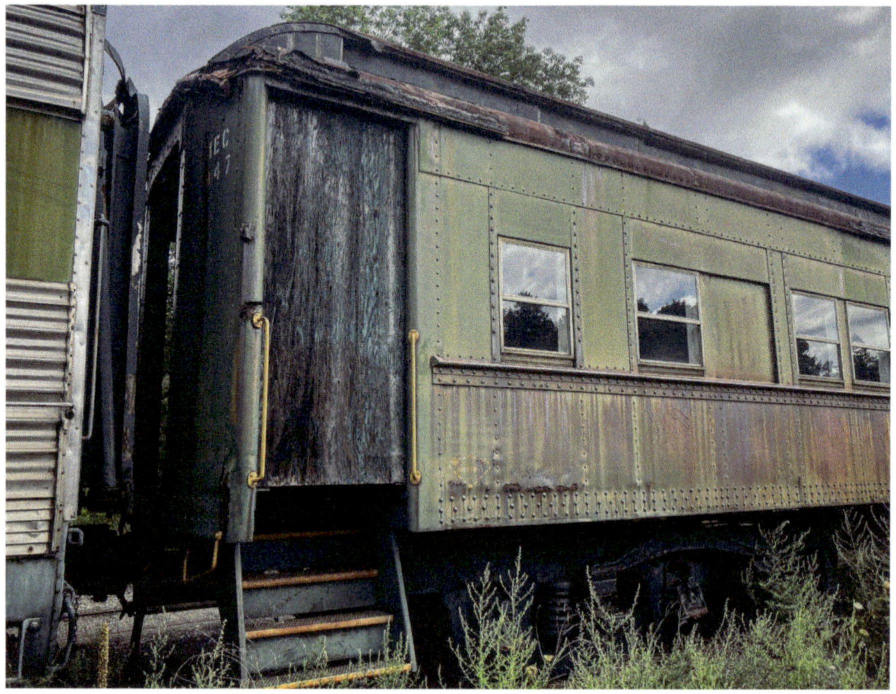

Originating from the 1930s, this coach, formerly designated as MEC #947, was repurposed into a Maintenance of Way (MOW) car prior to arriving at its current location.

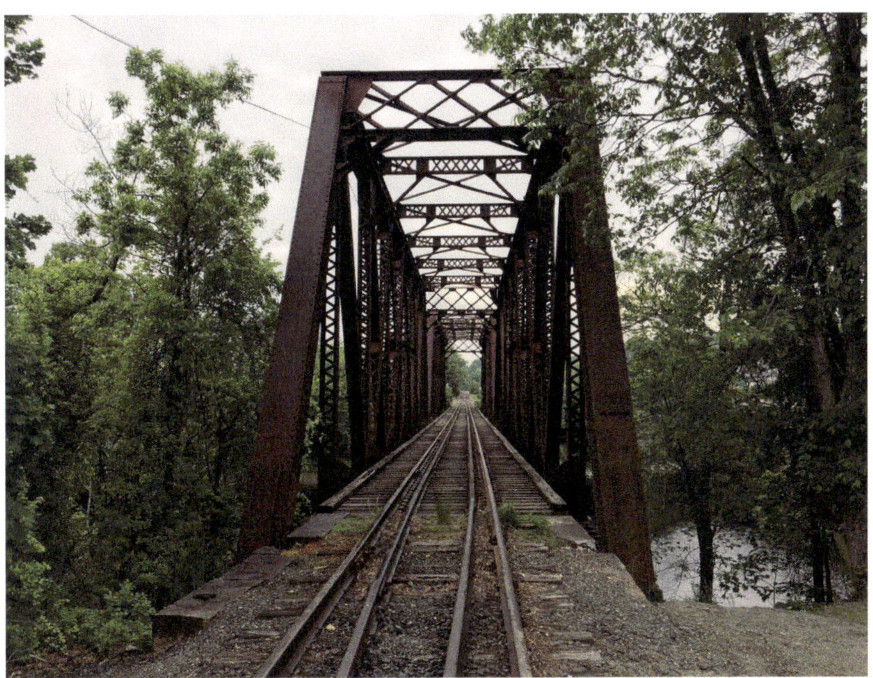

The Fort Halifax Train Bridge in Winslow, Maine, crosses the Sebasticook River and was constructed by the Pennsylvania Steel Company.

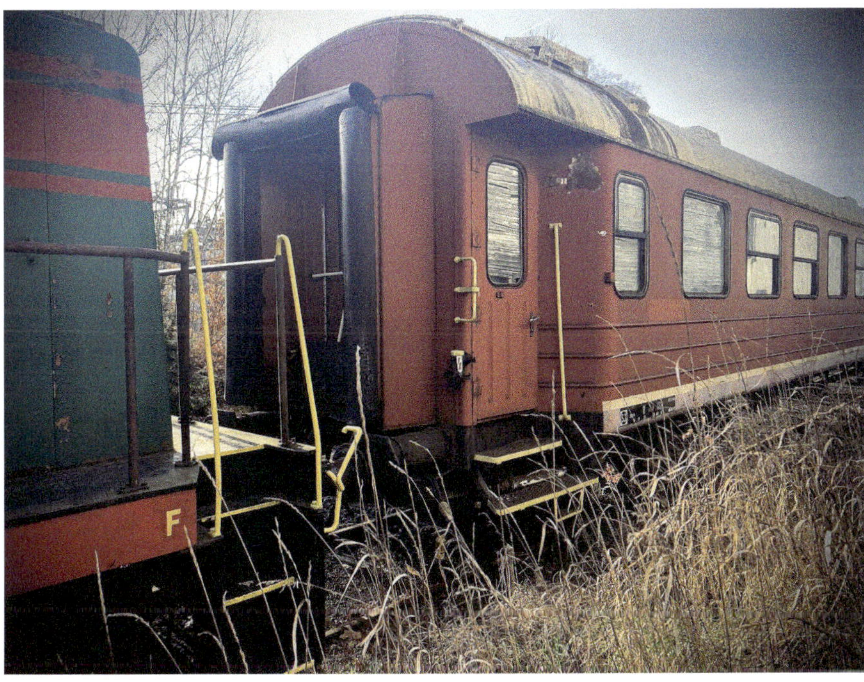

This standard coach from Swedish Railways was built in 1960. It sported a red livery and was equipped with air conditioning.

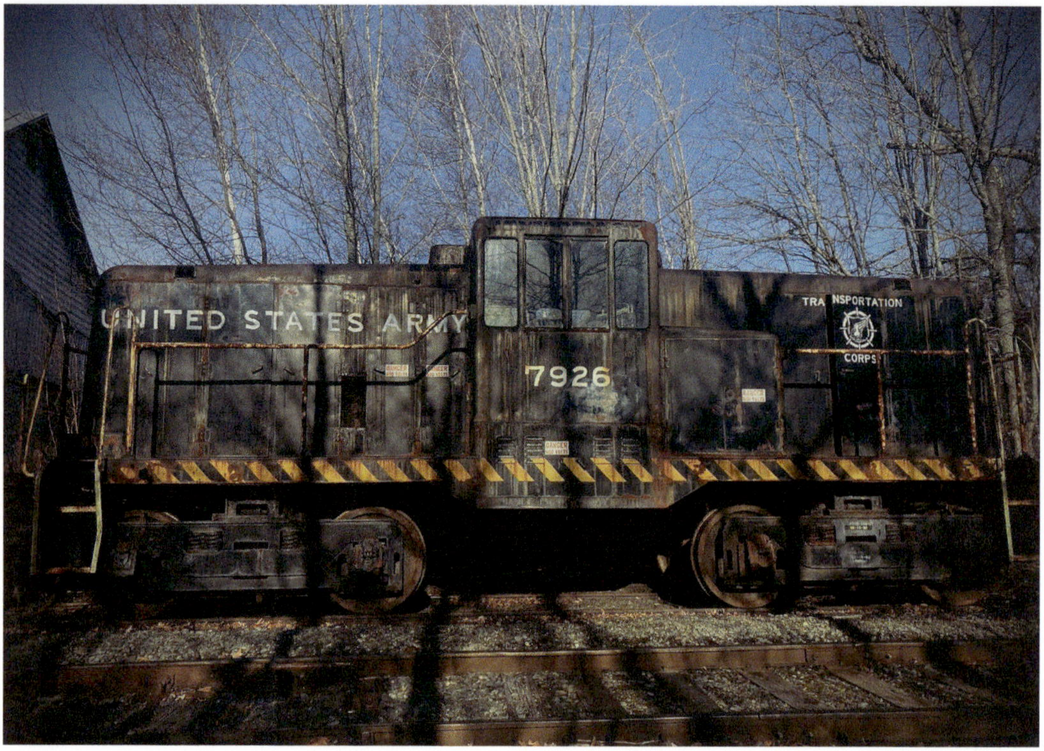

In 1944, General Electric manufactured a 45-ton center-cab switcher specifically for the United States Army.

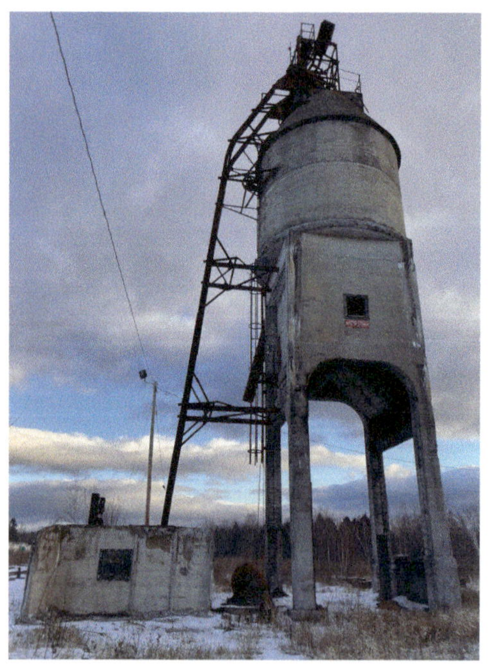

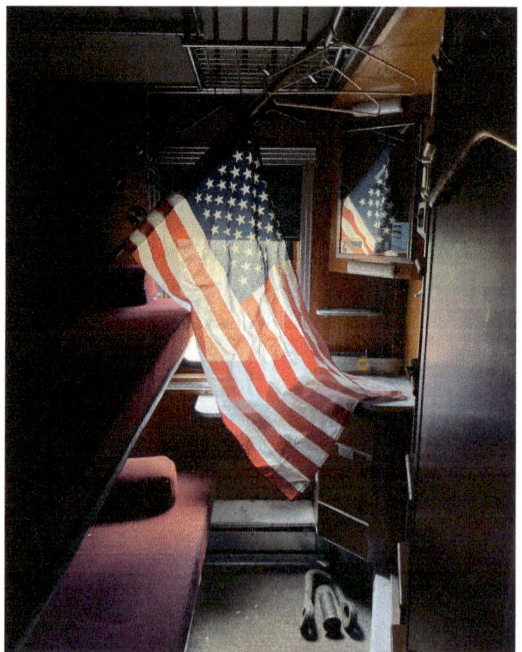

Above left: Perched in Millinocket stands a weathered coal tower, constructed by the Ross and White Company.

Above right: This American flag endured the passage of time within this antiquated passenger car.

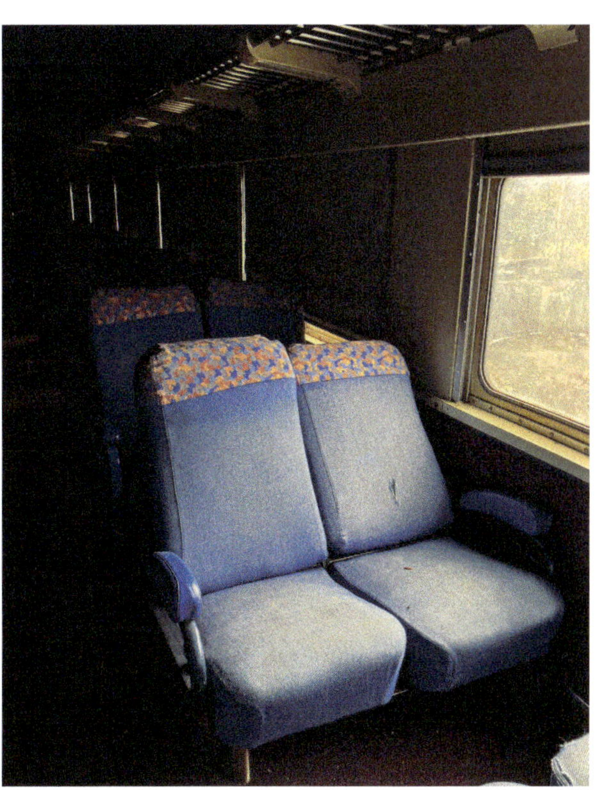

From a window seat, one could observe the scenery outside.

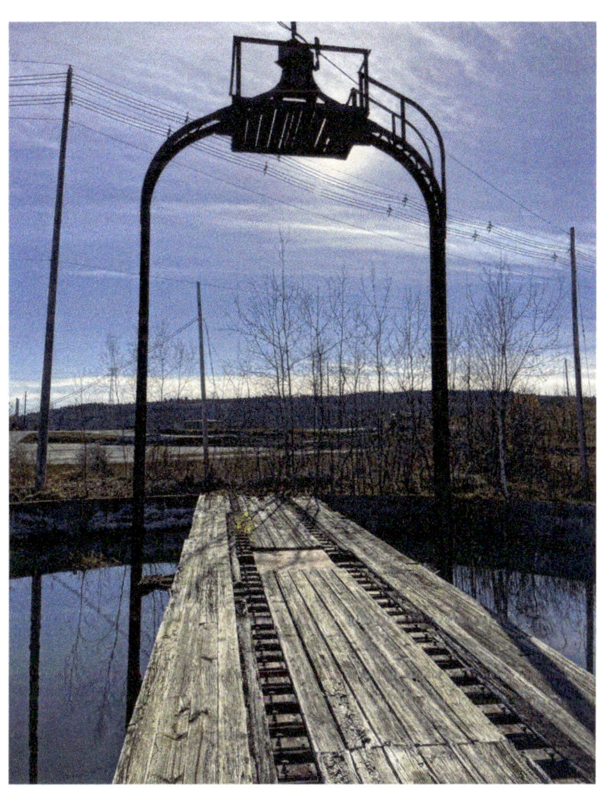

This image shows a turntable that was once utilized by the Bucksport paper mill.

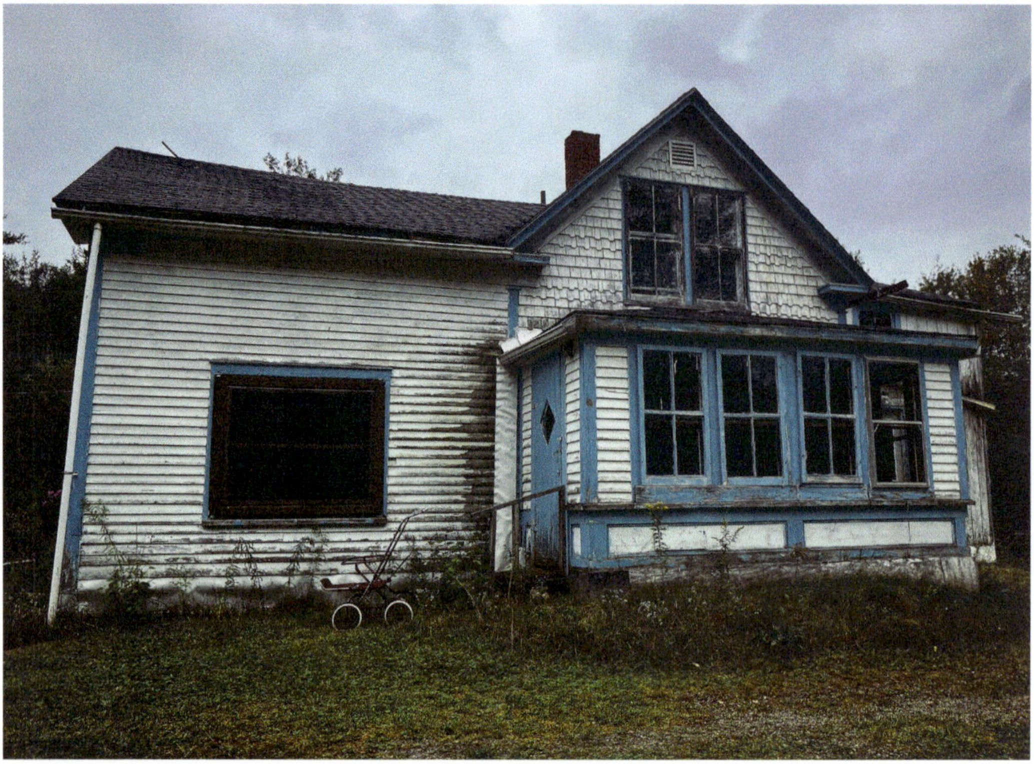

At the terminus of a disappeared track, a train conductor's house stands in quiet solitude.

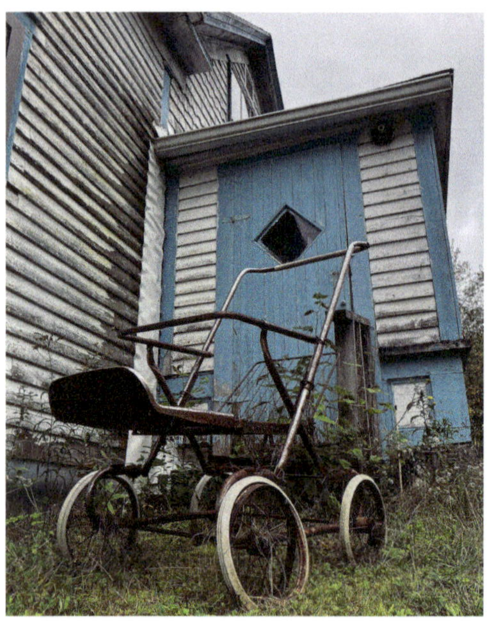

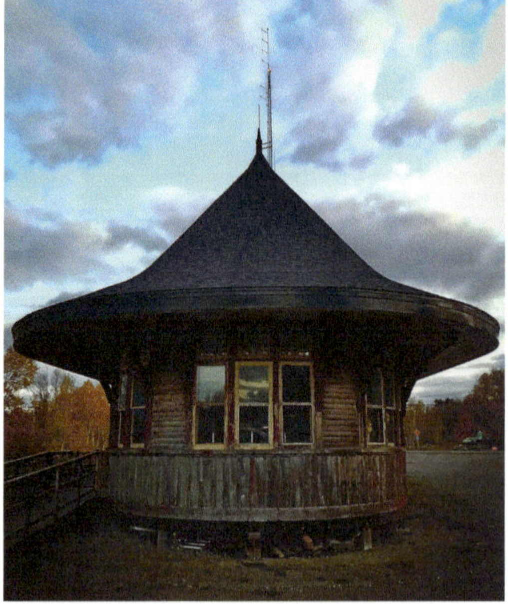

Above left: An old-fashioned baby stroller creates a picturesque scene, highlighting the juxtaposition of the vintage elements.

Above right: A train station in Northern Maine sits patiently, waiting to be preserved.

10

ELAN

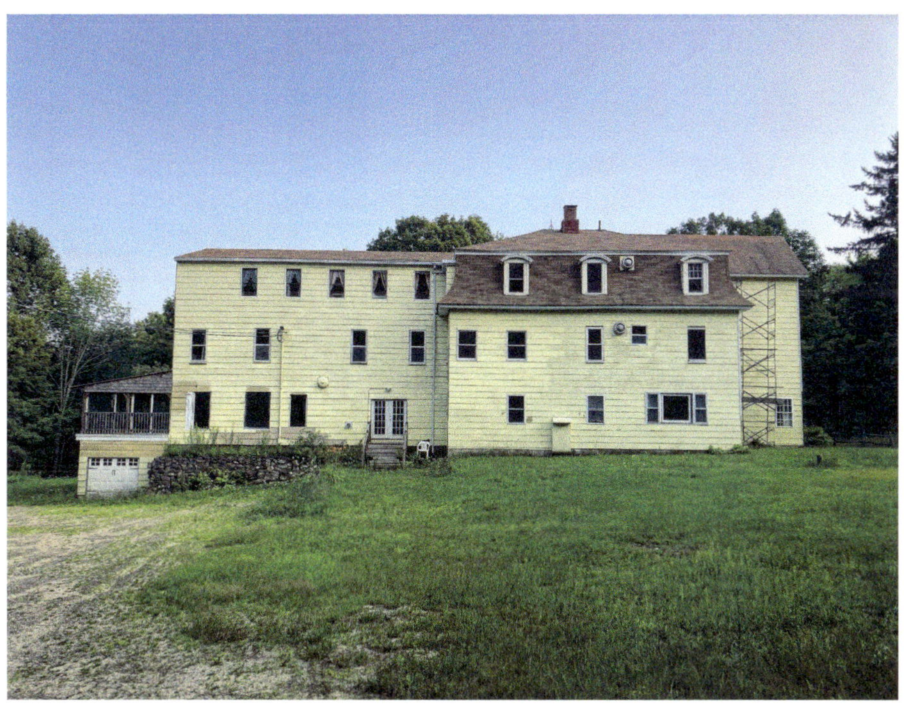

Here lies the old lodge, known to most as Elan.

Nestled deep within the mountains of Parsonsfield, Maine, lies a historic structure that was built in 1883 and originally known as the Forest Lake Lodge and Cottage. This summer hotel was operational from June 1st to October 1st with C. C. Varney as proprietor. Rates of board varied per occupant depending on the size and location of the room. A single person was charged eight to twelve dollars, and a double occupant was required to pay anywhere between fourteen and twenty-one.

By the year 1900 it had been renamed and was operating as the Maple Crest Hotel. This high end, charming retreat sat on multiple acres of land advertising twenty large rooms to rent plus their cottages surrounding the hotel. A large maple grove was within a short walk. If on the hill facing the house, the White Mountains could be seen. Mountain climbing, driving, fishing, and more were offered there along with an experienced culinary department that provided a home table with vegetables and milk from an adjoining farm.

Established in 1911, Dr. Francis Welch repurposed the hotel as a private sanatorium specializing in the treatment of tuberculosis and respiratory illnesses. Renamed as Maple Crest Sanatorium, the facility boasted modern amenities such as steam heating and rigorous sanitation practices, attracting patients seeking healing in its serene surroundings.

Dr. Welch's reputation for providing high-quality care attracted patients from far and wide, with some families choosing the sanatorium for its access to pristine spring water and locally sourced fresh produce. Following World War I, Welch entered into a contract with the Veterans Administration to treat veterans suffering from lung diseases, prompting the renaming of the facility to Rest Land Sanatorium. Despite his dedicated efforts, Dr. Welch passed away in the late 1950s, leaving behind a legacy of compassionate healthcare. Following his passing, the lodge underwent a series of transformations, serving as a sportsman's lodge, Randall Mountain Lodge, and briefly as Stow Restaurant. However, a significant chapter in its history unfolded when the property was repurposed in 1975 as a school for troubled teens under the ownership of the Elan One Corporation.

Despite the fond memories held by locals of the lodge's days and as a restaurant adorned with town themed murals, whispers of dark secrets and hidden truths lingered within its walls. Rumors circulated about the facility being a place for children with extreme behavioral issues, with chilling tales of a basement jail cell reserved for the most severe cases. Intrigued by these stories, I ventured inside, uncovering the truth about the past and confronting the haunting reality of the alleged jail cell. Before I knew it, I was interviewing an Elan alumnus who had expressed a preference for spending more time in the jail cell then the three months he already served, rather than returning to school upstairs.

During my teenage years, tales spread about an abandoned mental asylum where teens would escape to party on the weekends. Little did they know, the truth was far darker—it was actually a state lockdown facility for troubled teens. Within these walls, a harrowing reality unfolded. The teens housed there faced abuse from fellow students and staff, both mentally and physically. The facility employed coercive tactics, aiming to "straighten out" the teens through forced confrontations and punishments, instilling fear and control.

Elan, comprised of multiple schools across the state, harbored disturbing incidents of violence and tragedy. The environment of fear and manipulation escalated further, after new arrivals were subjected to disorienting and frightening experiences, blindfolded and abruptly taken from their childhood beds in the dead of night without explanation. At one school in Poland, a student tragically lost his life after a brutal boxing ring was organized by teachers, where students were pitted against each other.

The accounts of abuse and trauma that emerged from these facilities were gut-wrenching. Stories surfaced of a girl attempting to flee Elan, only to meet a horrendous death similar to the other student mentioned above. The difference was that she made it out alive, but died in another state after a truck driver raped and killed her. Another runaway, who was a fifteen-year-old boy at the time, was fatally shot in the heart by a local man. Security measures at these facilities included guards stationed in the woods, ready to chase down and apprehend any teens attempting to escape, reinforcing a culture of seclusion and control.

The disturbing legacy of Elan and its affiliated schools serves as a stark reminder of the vulnerability and mistreatment that can occur when unchecked power and manipulation intertwine within institutional settings. In the harrowing environment of Elan, children faced a cruel reality where even their attempts to seek help and contact their families were thwarted. Desperate to reach out and share their struggles, some teens would write letters home, only to discover later that their messages never reached their parents. If they were on the phone and said something "out of line" their conversation would end abruptly.

The staff at Elan maintained a tight grip on all communication in and out of the facility, scrutinizing every letter, ensuring that only information aligning with their oppressive tactics were allowed to pass through. Any messages that deviated from the facility's control mechanisms were swiftly destroyed, leaving the children isolated and unheard. As I navigated through the halls, I encountered murals that stood the test of time, one reflecting the lives that bore witness to the tumultuous history of the facility during its tenure as a school for troubled teens.

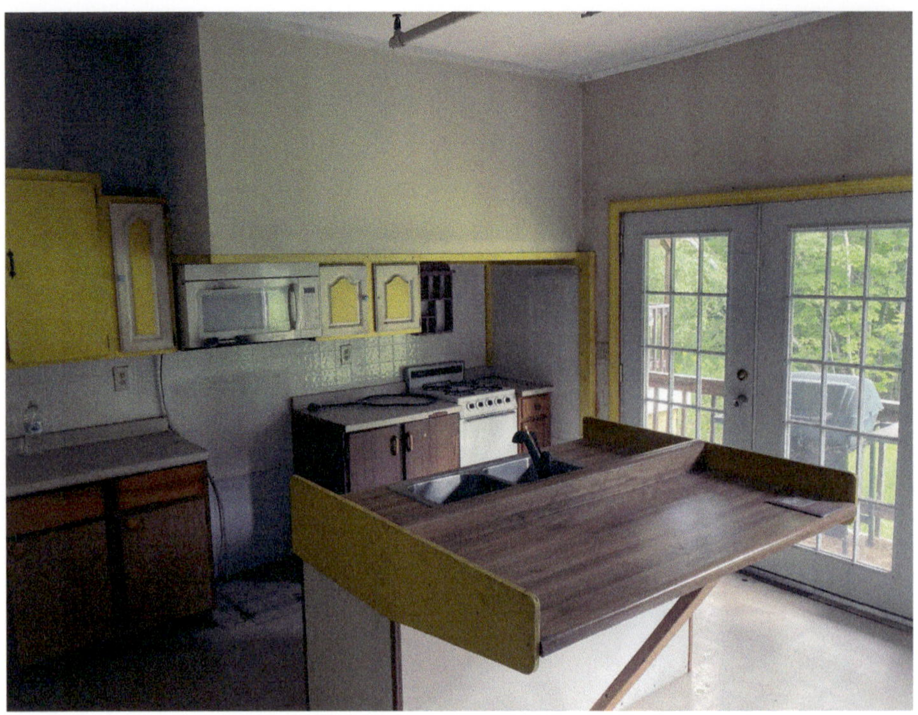

The kitchen featured a unique set up with a double bowl sink that also served as a dining area on the other side.

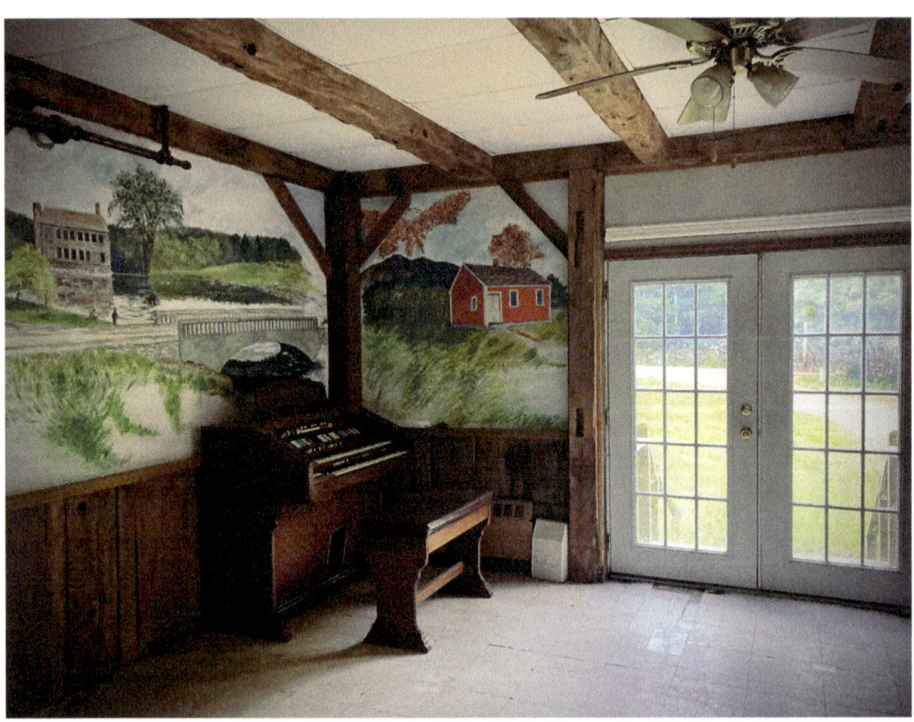

An elegant organ sat in the corner, patiently waiting to be played.

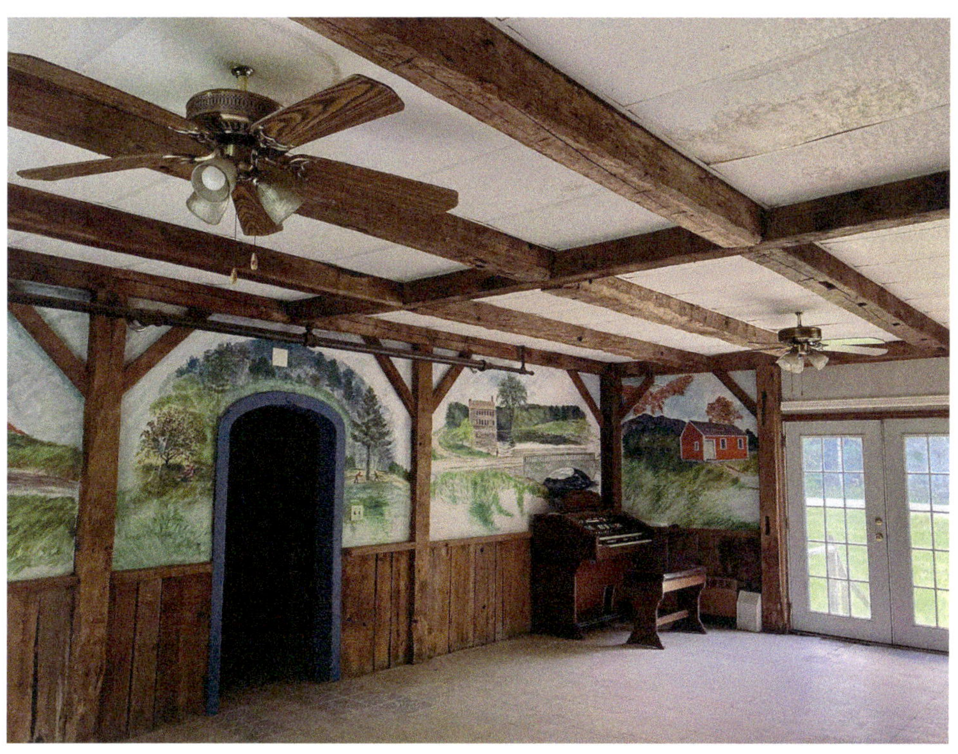

These murals were concealed when Elan was functioning as a school according to a past student.

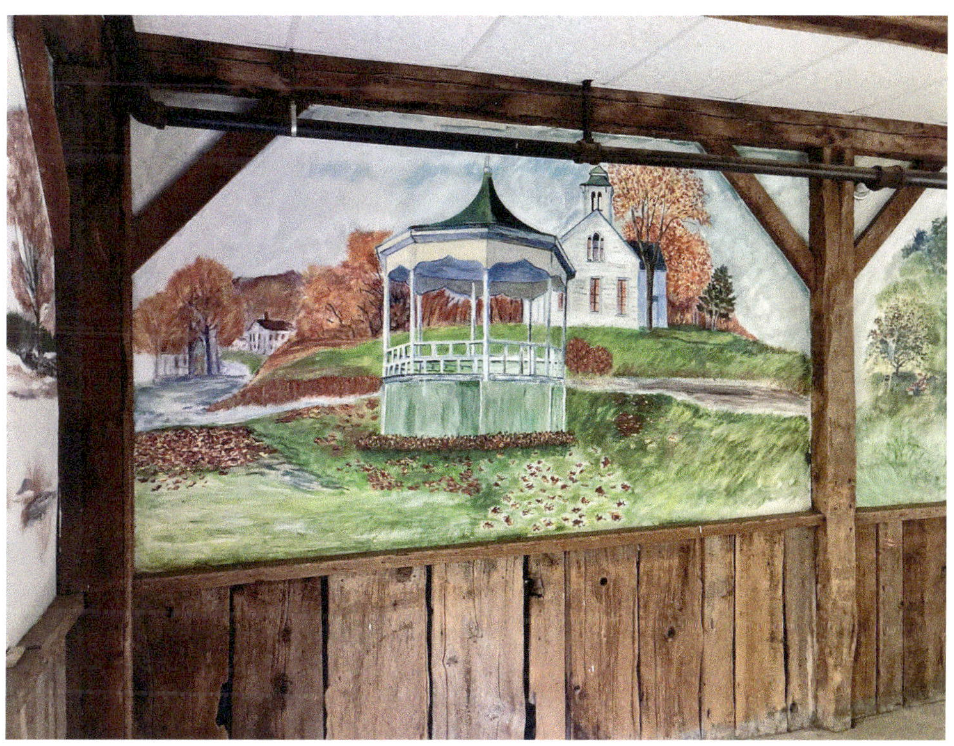

This close-up reveals the intricate details of this artwork.

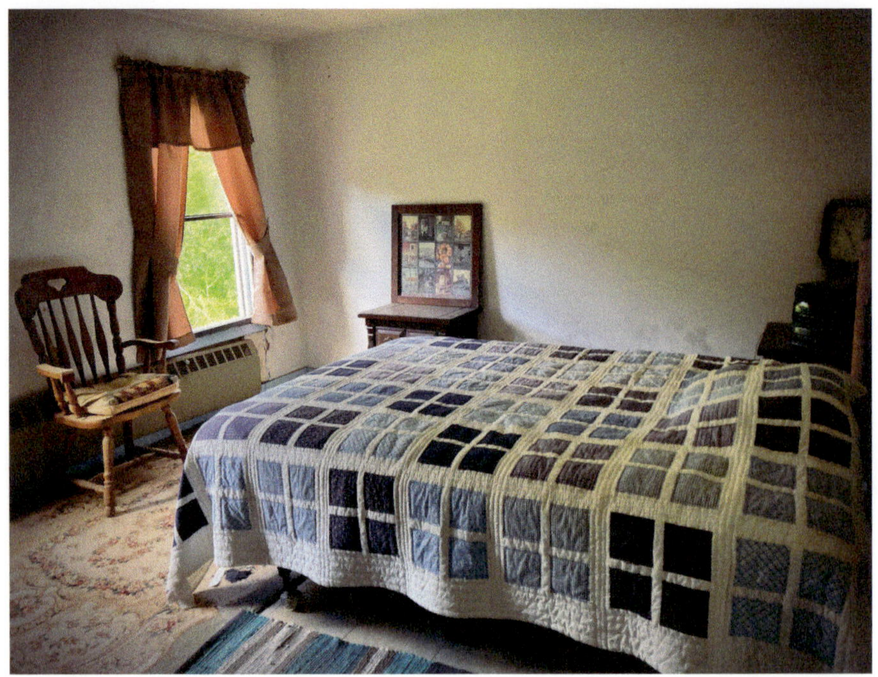

Furniture was left behind by the last family that lived here. After Elan shut down, it was then converted into a private residence.

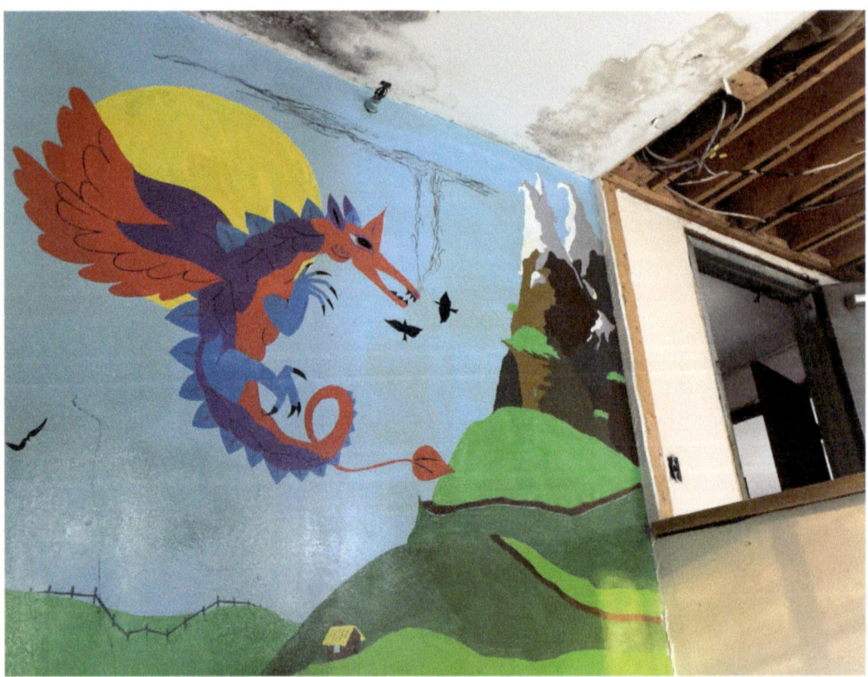

I'm unsure who painted the dragon mural, but I see a correlation with the children of Elan feeling trapped in the mountains of Parsonsfield, Maine. The vast mountains depicted in this painting could symbolize the sense of isolation and frustration among students. Even the dragon, with its wings, may not be able to fly high enough to escape, reflecting the captivity felt by the children.

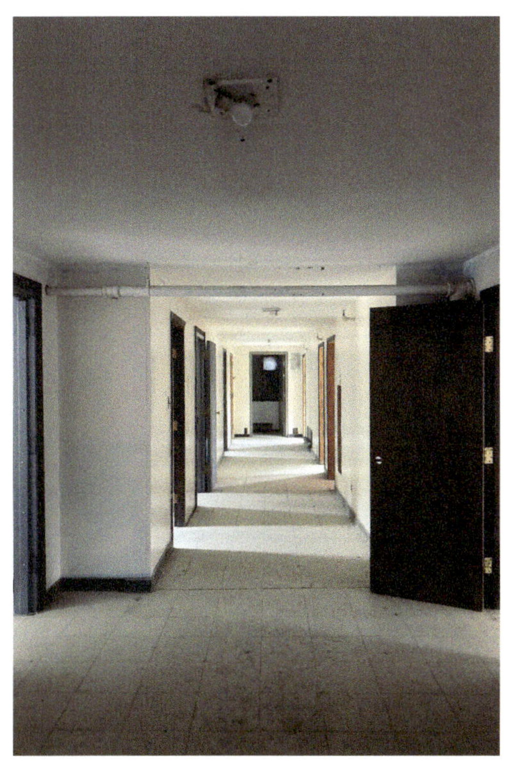

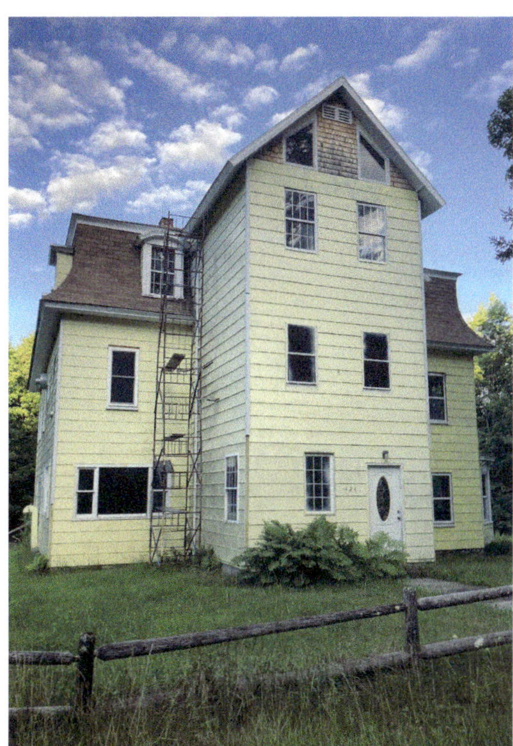

Above left: The vacant hallway looked quite dreary.

Above right: The staging to the left of the building was built out of the old bed frames that used to be inside.

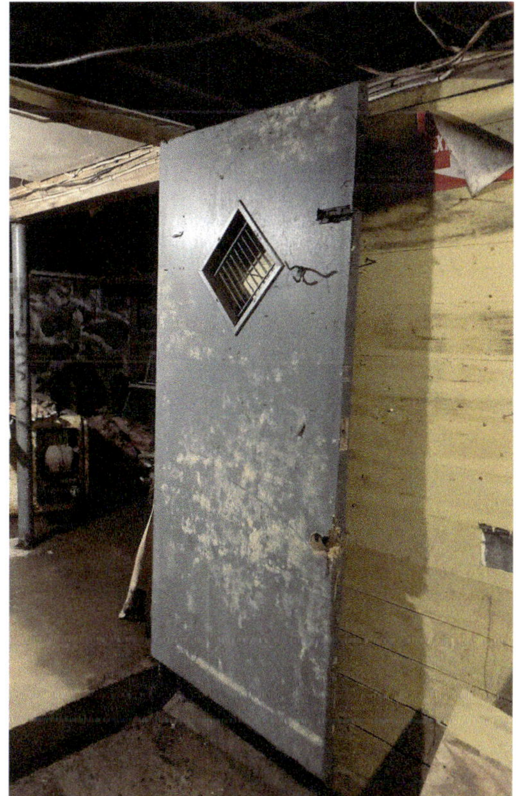

Right: This spot was used as a jail cell for the alleged unruly children. I spoke with an alumnus who had been forced to stay in there for three months.

11

THE FORGOTTEN HOMESTEAD

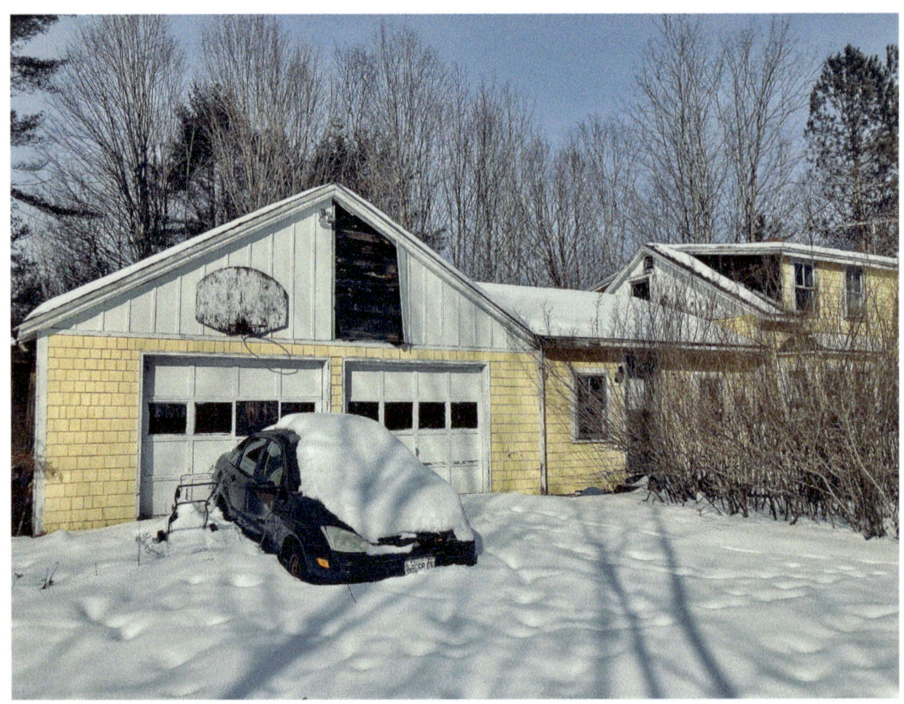

A car and a neglected basketball hoop sit idle in front of this house.

Each exploration offers a chance to learn and discover intriguing artifacts. Most tend to evolve quickly and become outdated rather fast. Old traditions like marking your child's height on the inside of their bedroom door often get lost. Some, however, get frozen in time, such as at this house. Here, I stumbled upon a lock of hair intricately fastened with a string. Perhaps this was before the days of modern photography, and a mother wanted a souvenir of her child's first haircut. Maybe it was from a deceased loved one. Alongside it were employee railroad tickets from the 1900s, hinting at a family member's job. I uncovered a treasure trove in a large trunk, filled with pictures and journals, documenting a life of adventure and memories. Among the other personal belongings was also a clay pipe.

The house exuded a sense of past love, particularly evident in the music room embellished with a piano, organ, violins, and banjos. The instruments cast a nostalgic glow, with the violin resting in its original velvet-lined case. Despite the musty odor of mold that permeated the air, I immersed myself in the history until compelled to depart.

Evidence of the woman who lived here's legal profession emerged, hinting at her dedication through the photographs of her travels, possibly from the eighties or nineties. The album in the kitchen provided glimpses into her life, back when the exhilarating wait for film to develop was comparable to the excitement of unwrapping a Christmas gift. I remember anxiously waiting for both as a kid. Perhaps I also like to explore because it reminds me of a time when life moved at a much slower pace, back when handwritten letters to Grandma were a cherished tradition. Even now, I still find joy in continuing this heartfelt practice.

Venturing upstairs, I encountered four American flags bearing forty-nine stars, a unique historical find. One flag, sewn together with four others, hinted at a special purpose. A serendipitous discovery revealed an old sewing machine, accompanied by the woman's engraved name tag sitting on her desk, weaving together the narrative of the house's owner.

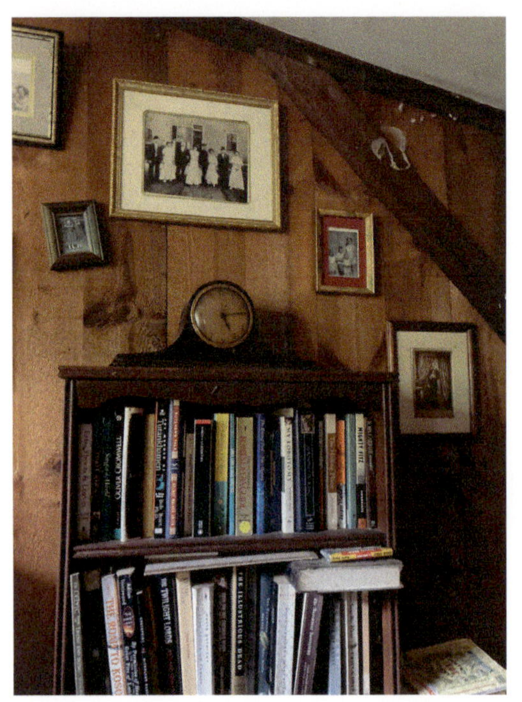

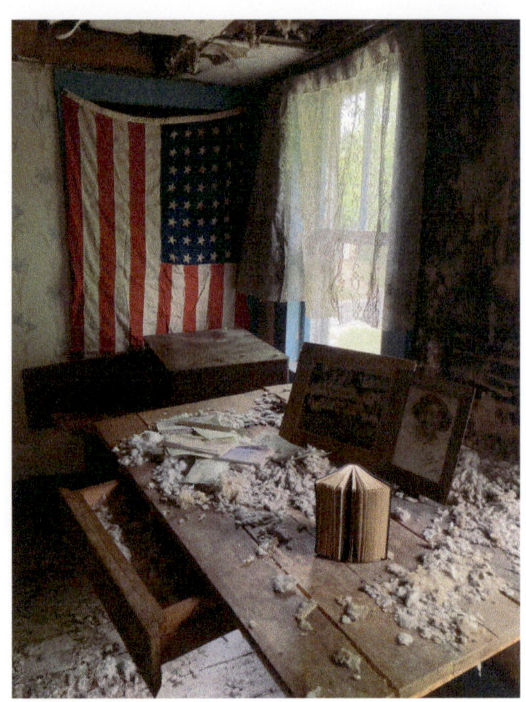

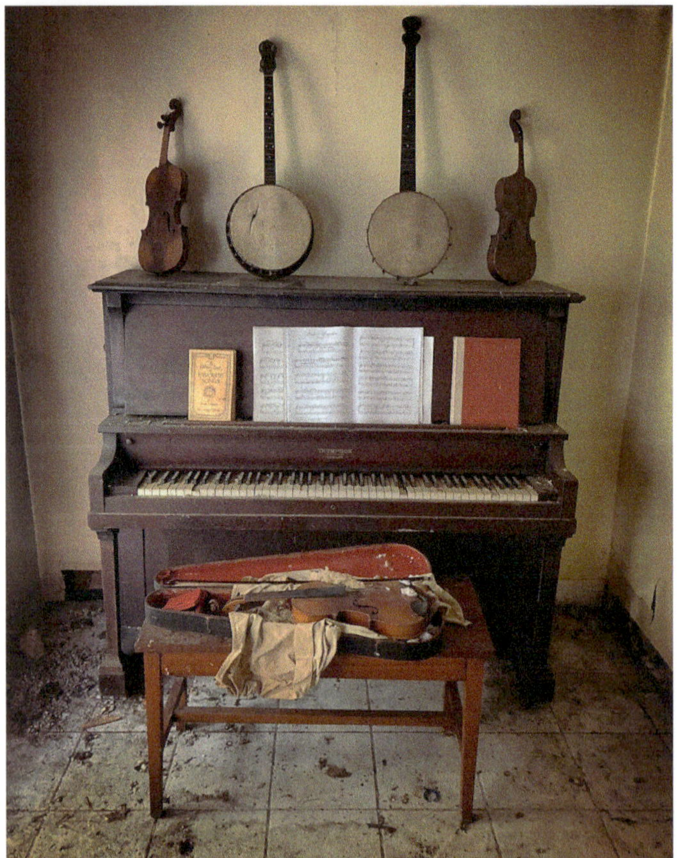

Above left: This house was decorated with an antique clock and photographs that seemed to defy the passage of time.

Above right: The lawyer's desk sits empty, with a sewing machine in the background.

Left: Musical instruments played a significant role in this household.

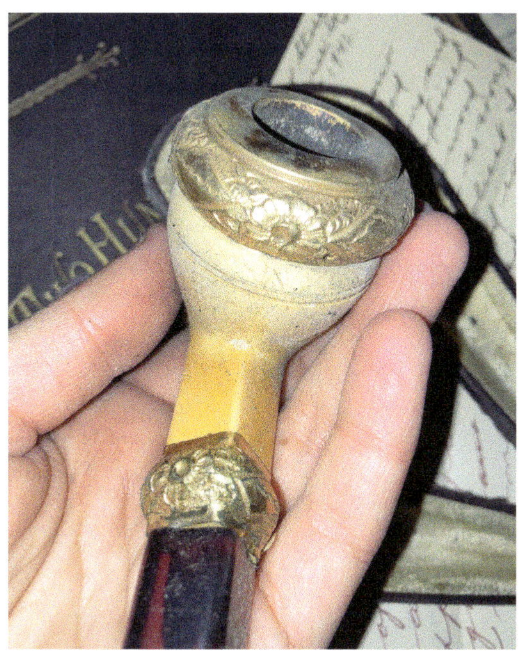

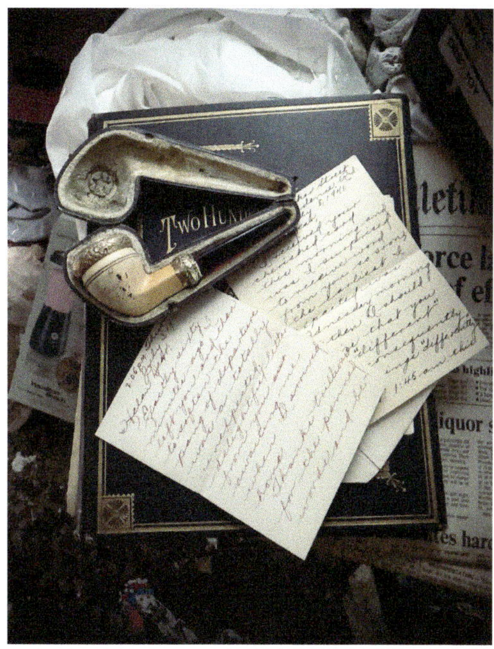

Above left: This clay pipe was meticulously crafted with intricate designs.

Above right: Displayed here is a clay pipe and correspondence exchanged between two lovers during World War II.

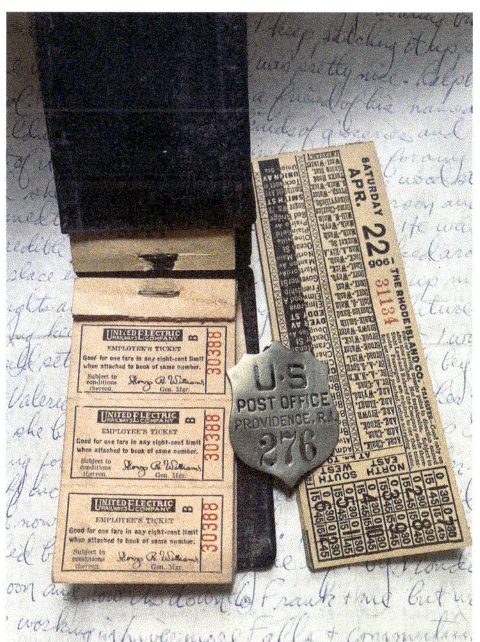

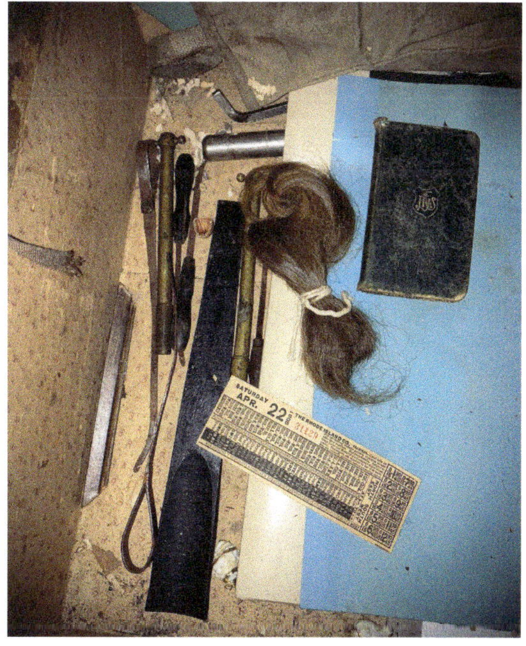

Above left: Train tickets dating back to 1905 were discovered, reflecting a time when trains were a prevalent mode of transportation. Notably, employee tickets were also found as you can see on the left.

Above right: While saving locks of hair may not be as common today, this practice has a long history and holds a deep significance for many people as a tangible connection to the past and their loved ones.

12

OLD RELICS AND AUTOMOBILES

The unpredictable nature of Maine's four distinct seasons means that you never know what type of vehicle or equipment you might stumble upon in the woods. From water slides to a Ferris wheel, and several old cars, I've come across a multitude of stuff. I've also found junk yards with several different types of antique vehicles, mostly built out of steel. One of my most cherished discoveries was a Checker Aerobus from the Kora Shriners. This unique vehicle was once used by the Shriners to travel to different towns and was even hand-painted, adding to its beauty. While the engine under the hood is now missing, it used to house a powerful 327 Chevy motor, reflecting its impressive build.

Growing up with my grandparents, who owned a junkyard, I witnessed my grandfather's unwavering passion for restoring vehicles, a hobby he continues to pursue at the age of eighty-six. I have fond memories of riding in his 1932 Ford Coupe and 1969 Chevelle that he rebuilt years ago, joining him and my grandmother in various town parades, including the parade for our hometown's annual fair. These vehicles also made appearances at car shows, where I spent countless hours with my grandparents, their friends, and fellow townspeople, listening to their captivating tales from the past.

In addition to exploring junkyards, I have also had the opportunity to visit an old paper mill that housed leftover motorcycles. Some of these old bikes were buried beneath the debris where a section of the mill had been torn down. On my initial exploration of the site, that section was still intact, but upon my return, most of it had been demolished, leaving only remnants of the first floor, the motorcycles, and a small gated-off area on the second floor. It was as if the back section had never existed, highlighting the impermanence of these structures. The fleeting nature of historical sites like this mill is one of the driving forces behind my desire to document and preserve these memories in writing. As time passes and the property is eventually demolished, there is a risk that in a century, people may never know that this place once existed.

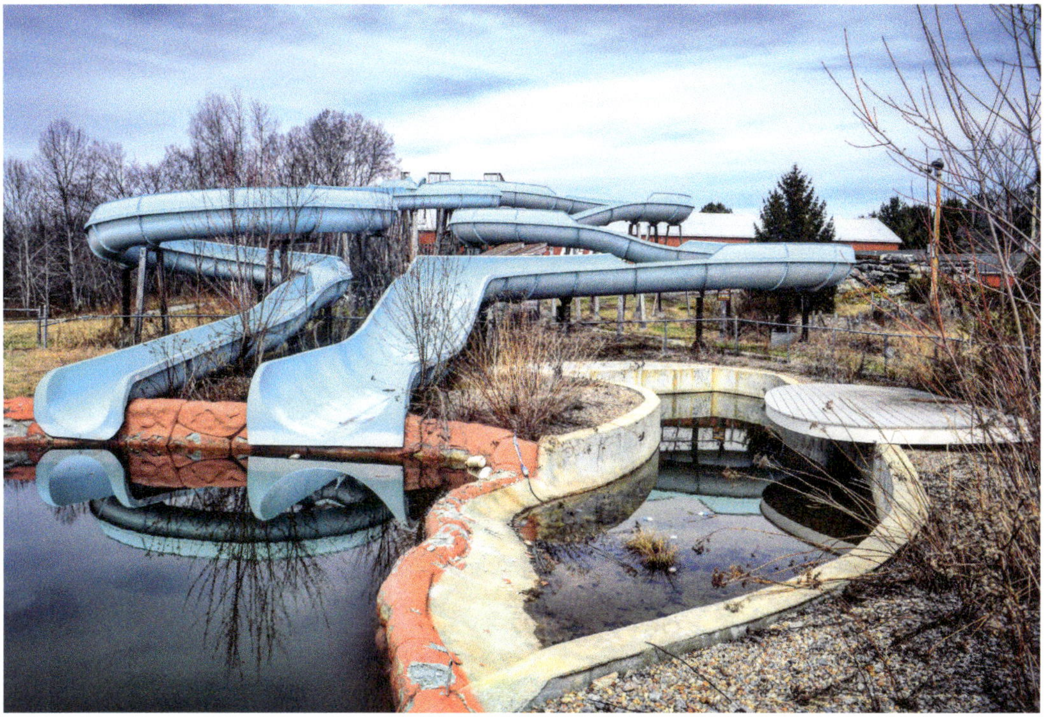

These water slides used to be the highlight of an adventure park in Bethel, but have now been removed. Following a renovation, the park has reopened without the water slides, for mini golf and ice cream.

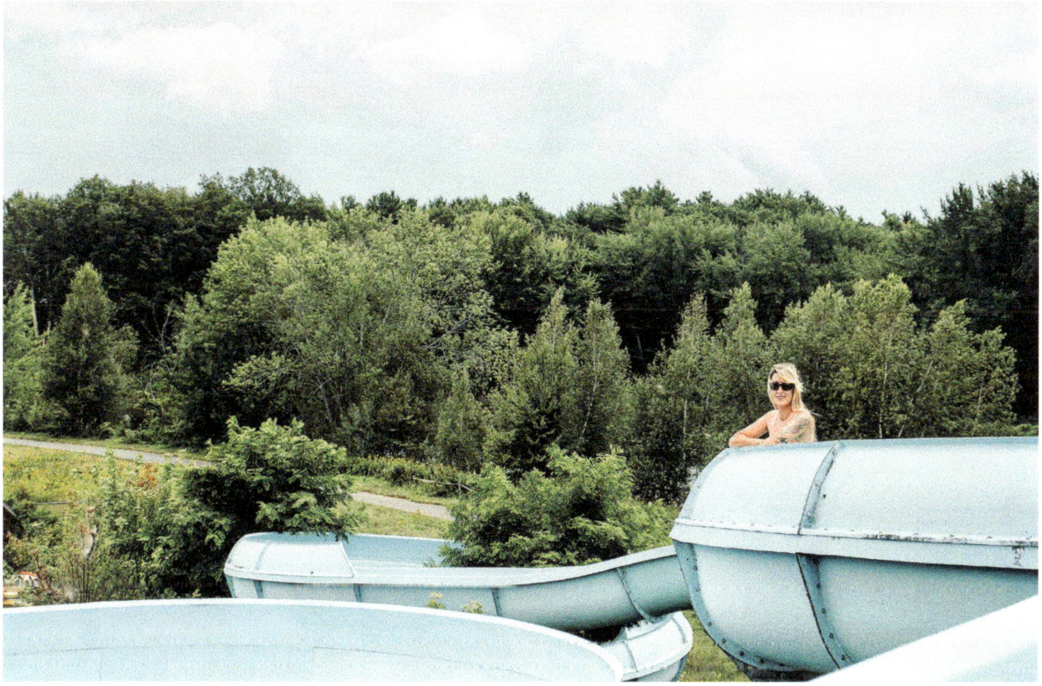

On this day I met up with Miranda and her friend. The time we spent exploring together was filled with joy and excitement. [*Miranda Dolph*]

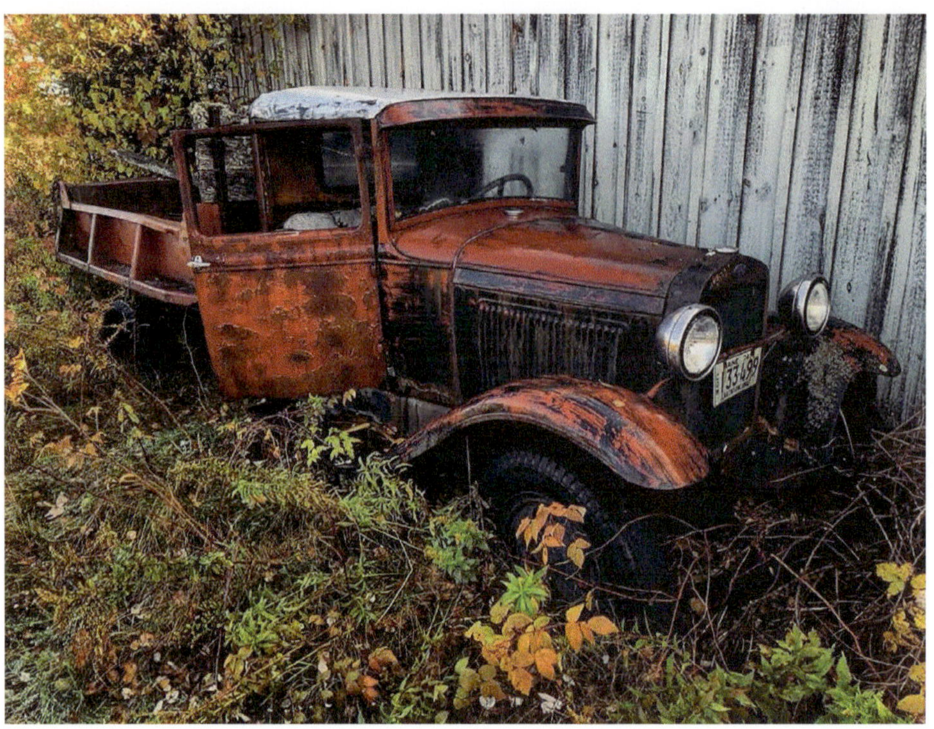

An antique Model AA rests quietly on a deserted airstrip.

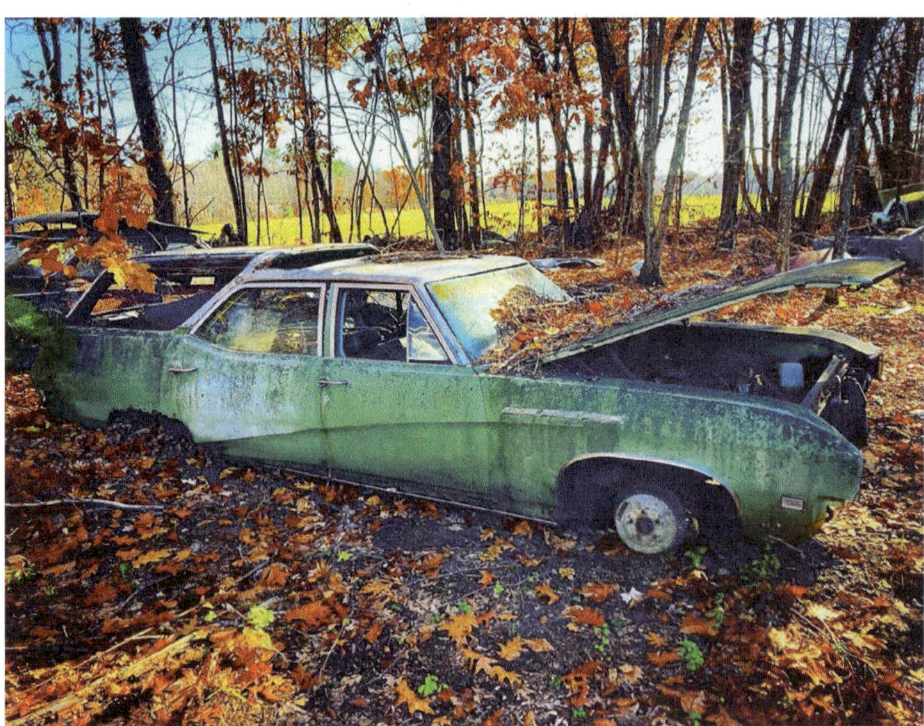

The Vista Cruiser stationed here awaits its transfer to a new home.

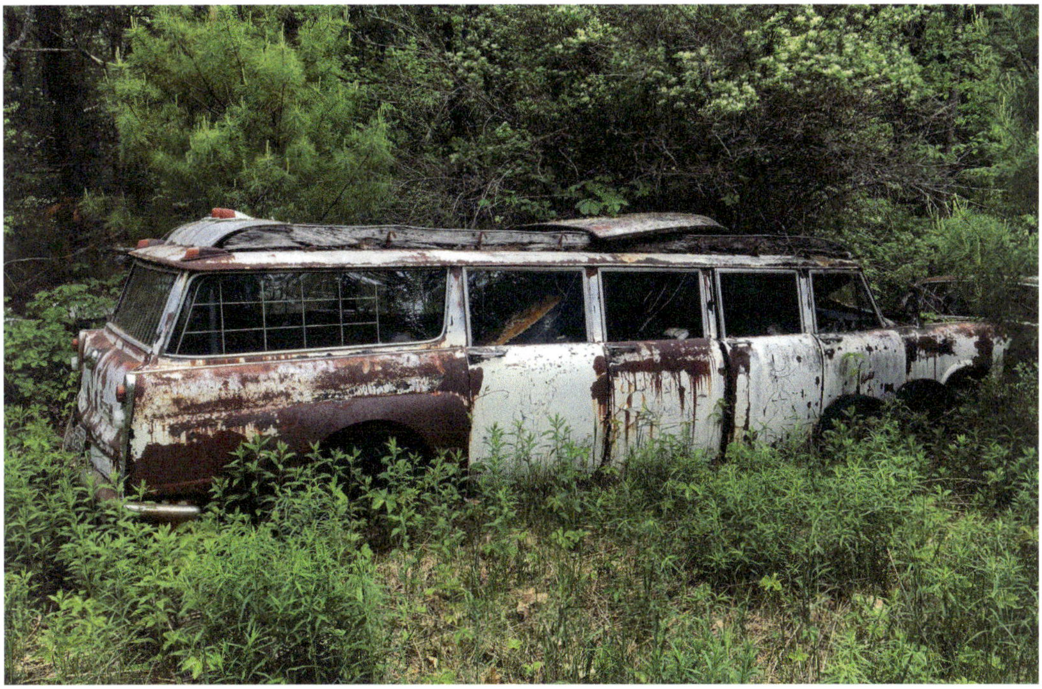

The Shriners utilized this Checker Aerobus for traveling between towns. It was meticulously hand-painted with care.

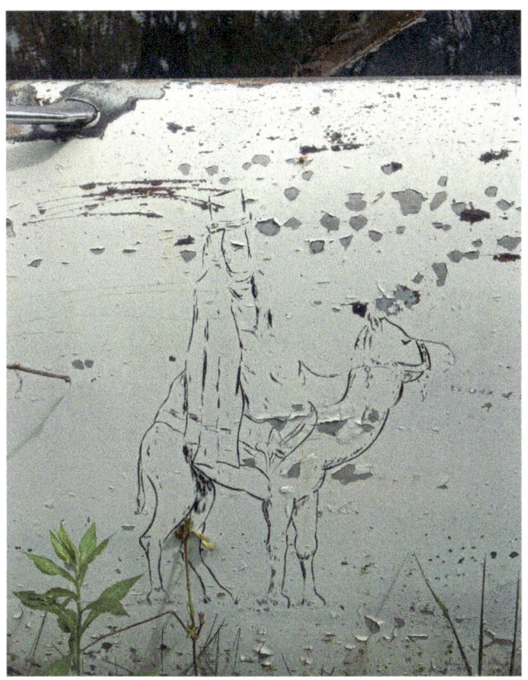

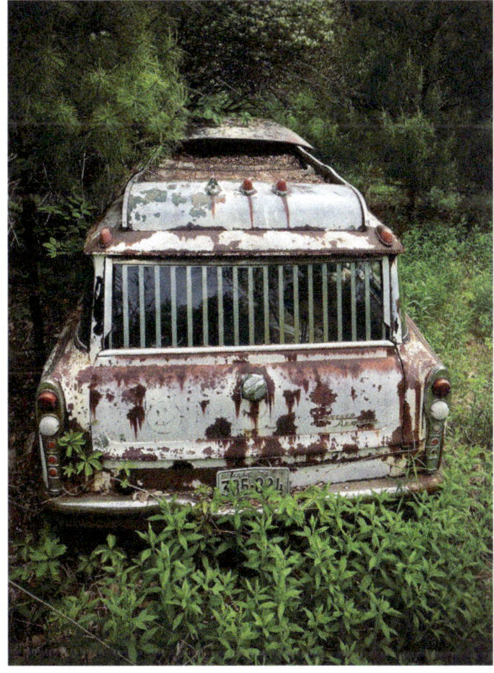

Above left: This picture depicts a close-up of the fourth passenger car door, hand-painted, showcasing someone riding a camel. This car has eight doors total.

Above right: The rear view of the Checker Aerobus.

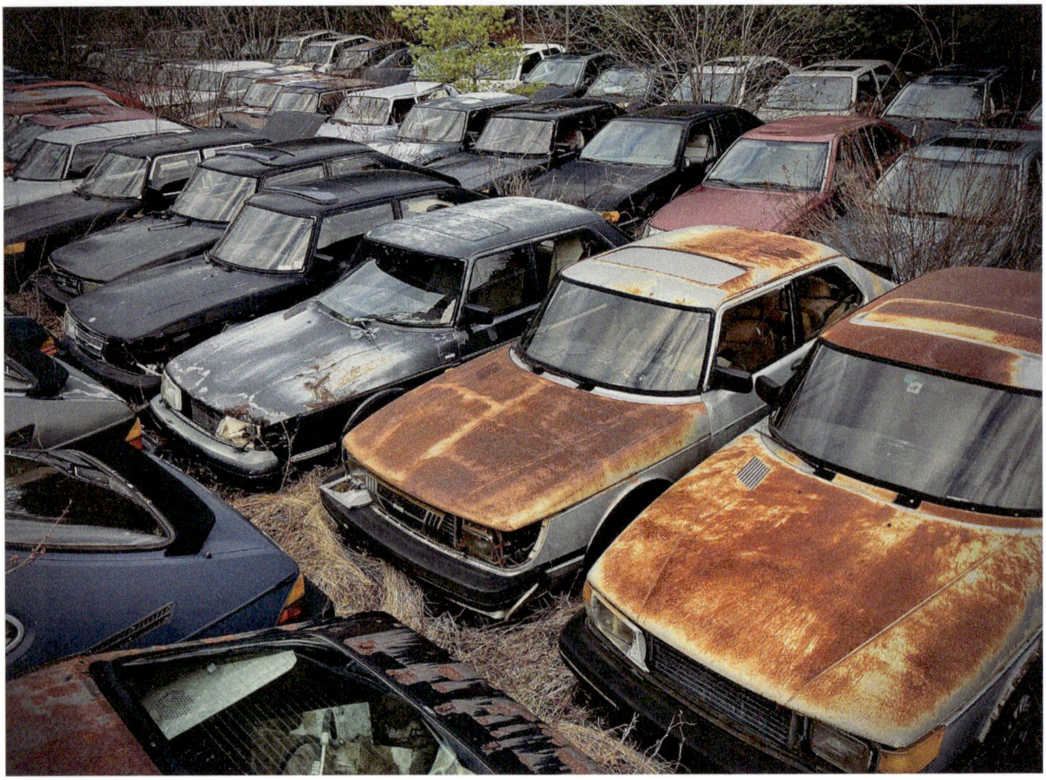

A Saab Graveyard!

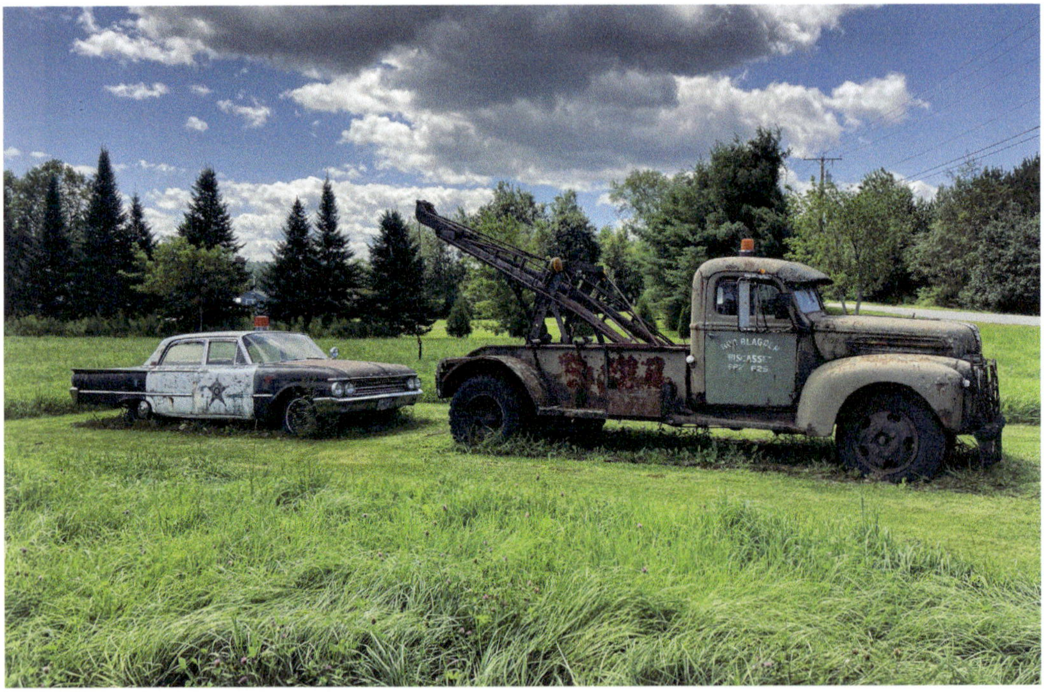

Pulled Pork!

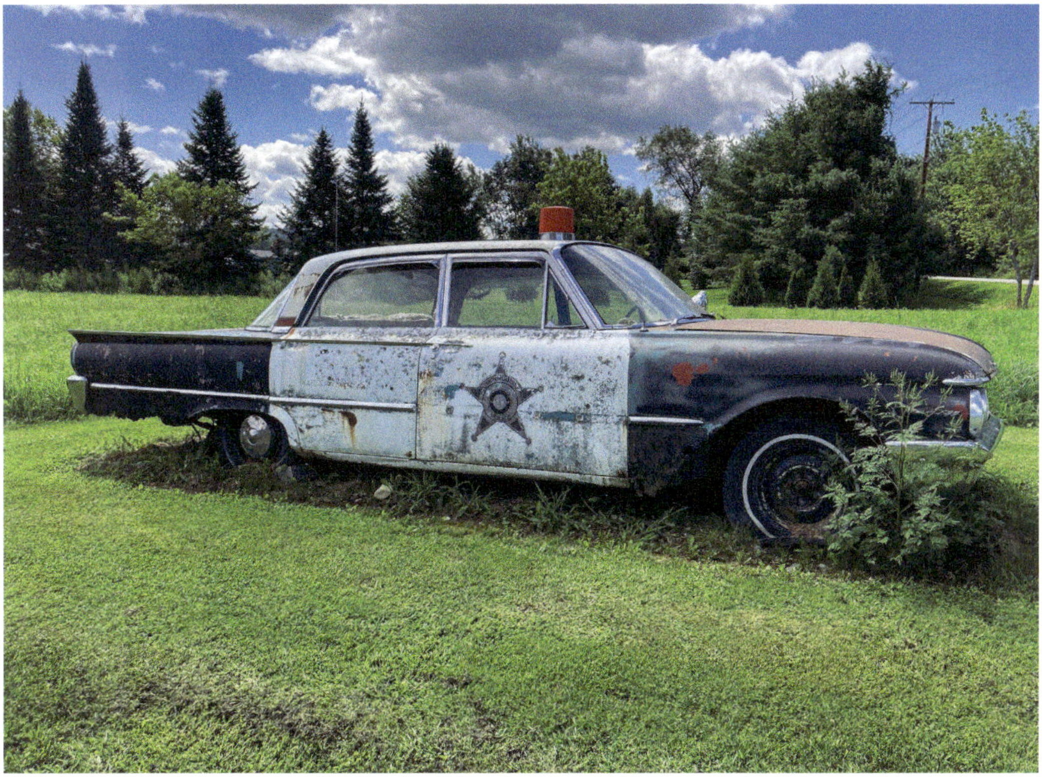

Pictured here is an old 1961 Ford Fairline that was used as a Monmouth Police car.

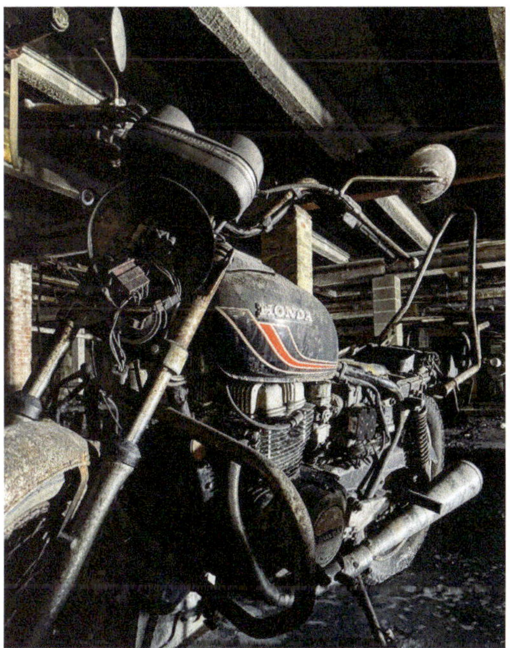

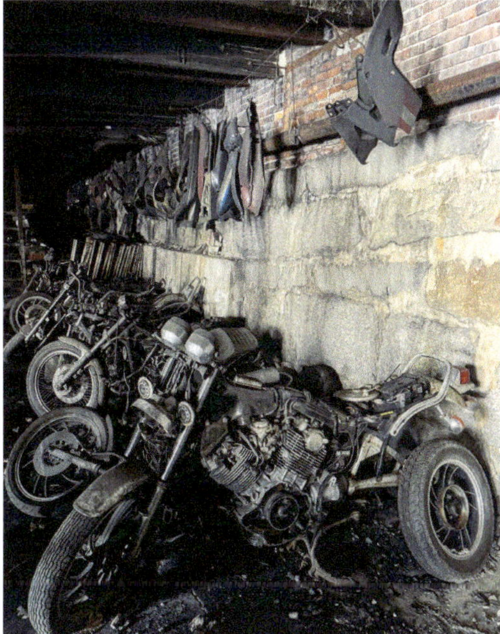

Above left: This old Honda stands gathering dust, snow, and any other debris that may come its way.

Above right: Numerous bikes are left to rot amidst the remnants of an old paper mill.

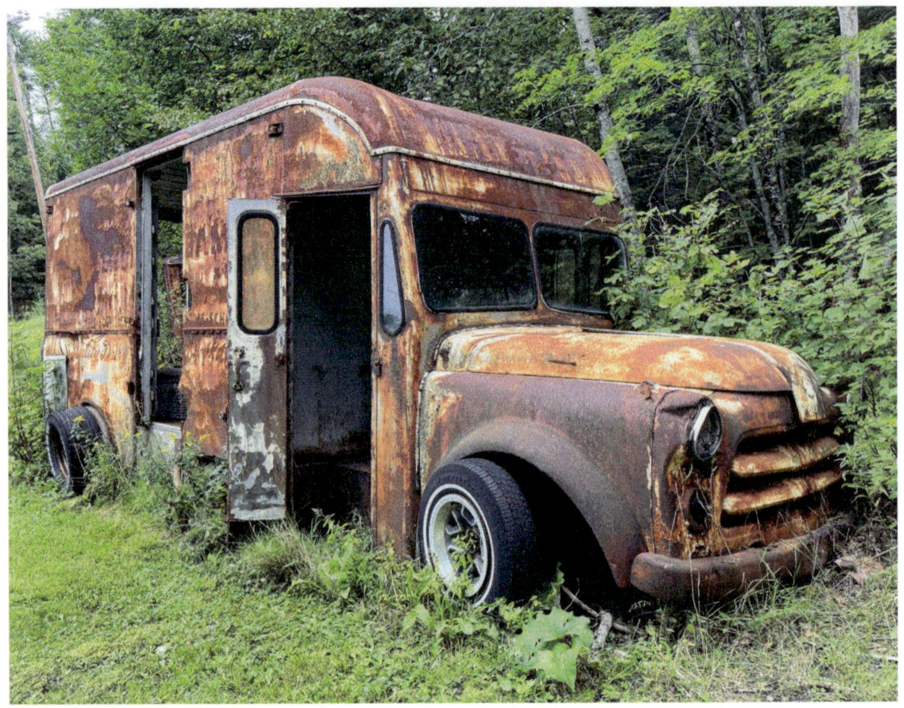

A vintage milk truck sits patiently, awaiting restoration near an abandoned railroad bed that has been reclaimed by nature.

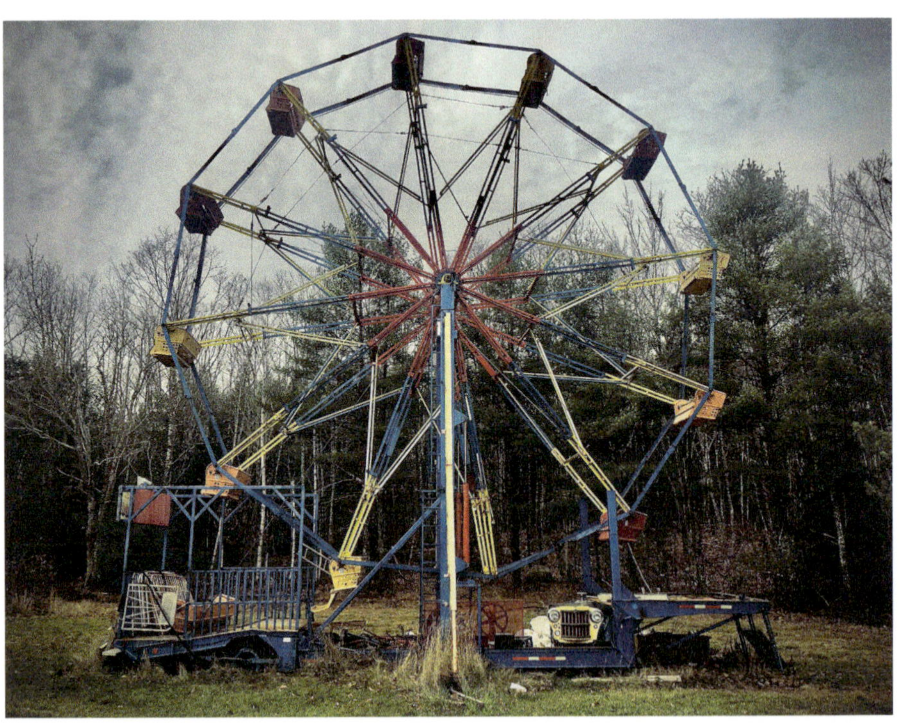

I have a great fondness for discovering unique and quirky items in the woods, which often provide insight about the personalities of their previous owners.

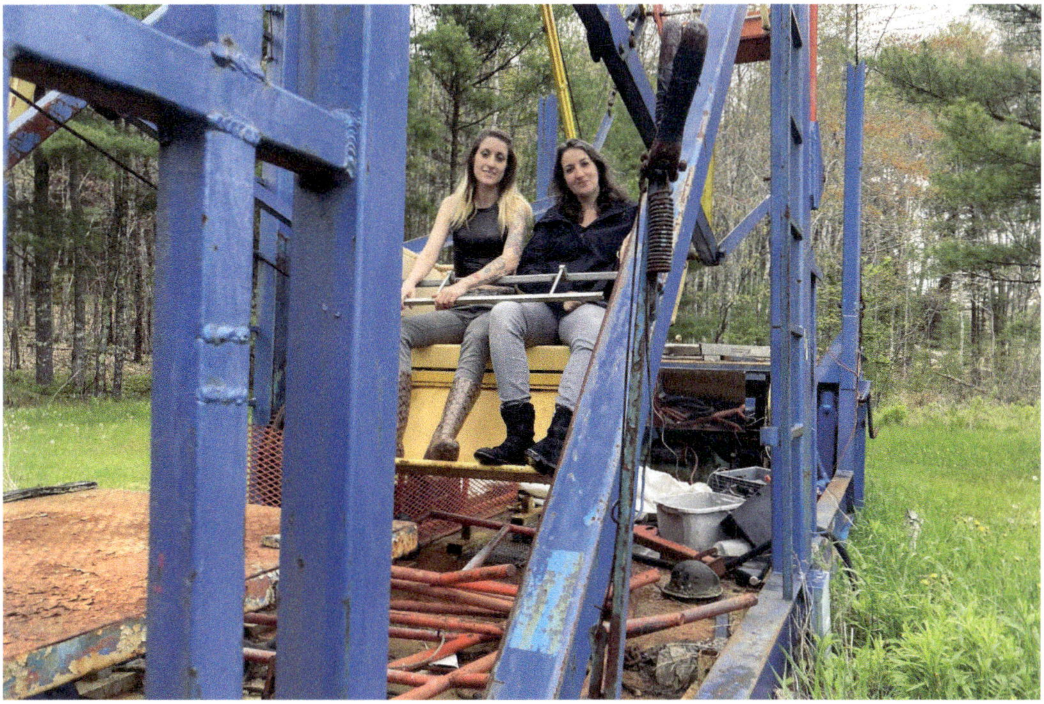

Discovering a Ferris wheel made me feel like a kid again. Excitedly, I hopped on with my friend, imagining what it was like when it was still in operation. [*Dale Peaslee Jr.*]

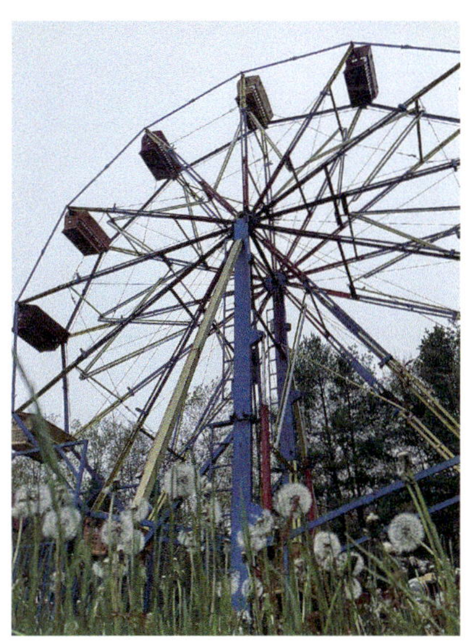

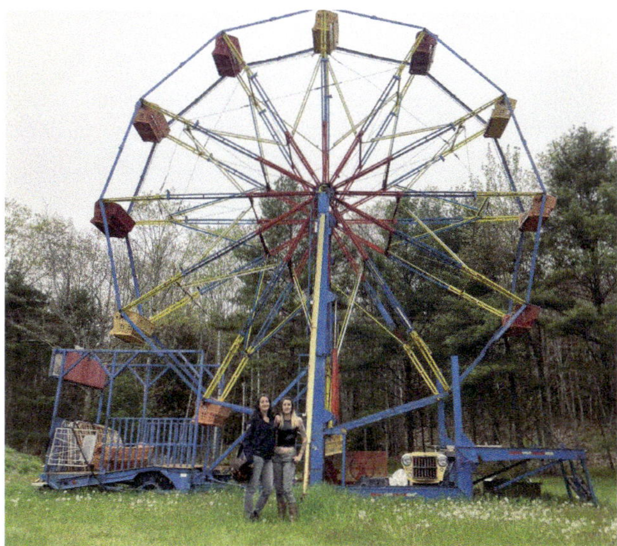

Above left: Coming to an abrupt stop, I seized the opportunity to capture this photo as the dandelions were on the cusp of releasing their seeds. In doing so, I not only offered viewers a distinct and unique perspective, but also drew a comparison to the idea of letting go of this abandoned structure.

Above right: My friend Diane and I made sure to get a picture with this treasure before it met its demise. Sadly, it has now been torn down. [*Dale Peaslee Jr.*]

ABOUT THE AUTHOR

Growing up in a household without siblings, Crystal Eastman discovered that solitude often sparked her creativity. From an early age, she immersed herself in artistic endeavors, finding joy in drawing, writing poetry, playing the keyboard, and helping her mother tie quilts. Over the years, she has composed numerous songs, poems, and short stories. Crystal's passion for writing and the great outdoors blossomed early on in life. At just twelve years old, she earned a scholarship to a hunter's safety camp after winning a writing contest with a piece about her first ice fishing experience alongside her father and a group of boys. During that memorable outing, she caught an impressive seven-pound, twenty-two-inch bass, as well as a four-pound bass on the same day, earning her recognition in the local newspaper and on the news.

After graduating high school, Crystal joined a promotional modeling team and made an appearance in a music video featuring a famous artist. She then pursued her dreams of acting and modeling with an agency in Florida. Since returning to Maine, Crystal has contributed her talents as a writer, model, and photographer to over thirty magazines, even gracing the cover of two. Most recently, she has embarked on a new creative path, exploring the state and photographing abandoned buildings that have succumbed to the passage of time. Driven by a desire to document Maine's history before it's lost, Crystal aims to share a glimpse into these once-vibrant spaces, inviting viewers to step inside a world that has been forgotten.

In addition to her photography, Crystal has been featured on IMDb, YouTube, and Amazon Prime, in both an interview and a television series. As a member of multiple historical societies, Crystal is passionate about uncovering the truth behind decaying buildings and seeking to understand the stories that lie within before they fade from memory.

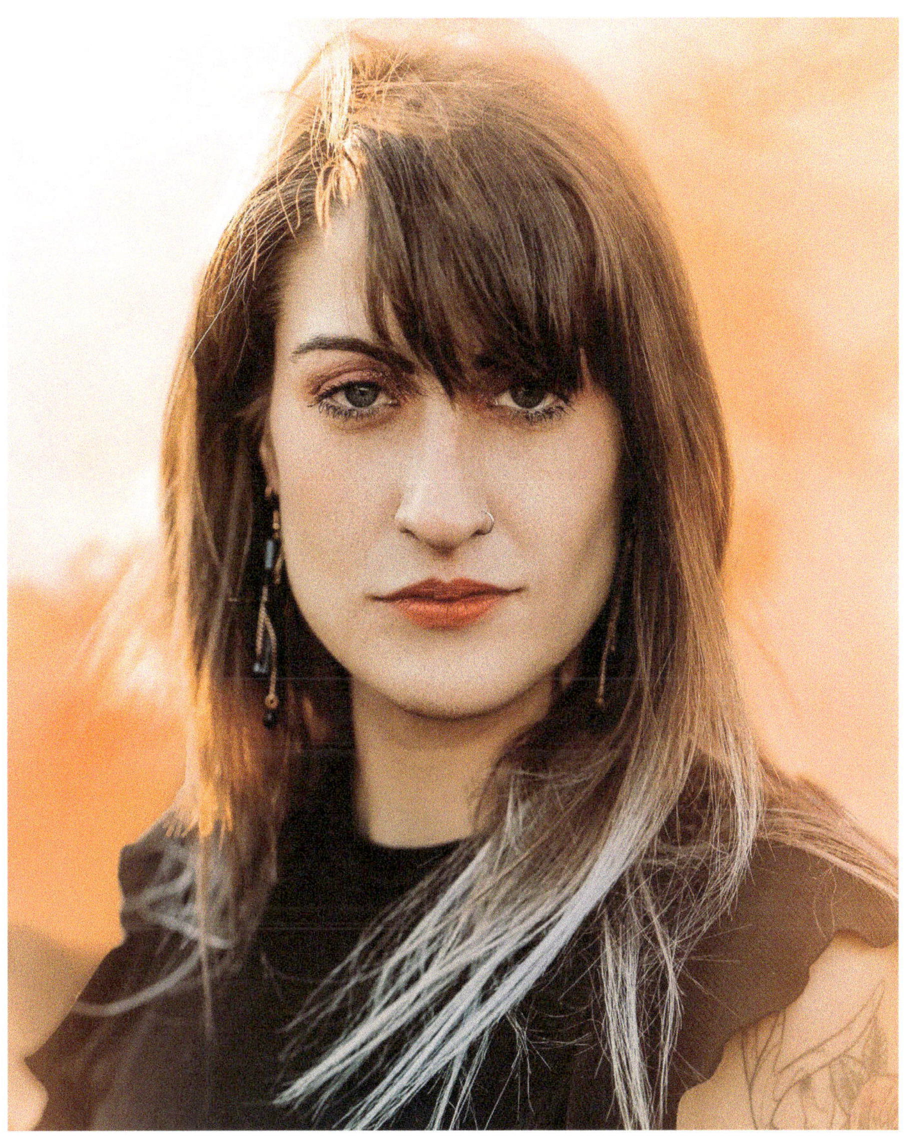

Please feel free to check out more of my work on Instagram @bandobabe207.
Thank you for reading my book. I hope that you enjoyed it! [*Patrick Gildard*]

BIBLIOGRAPHY

Davis, B., Mitchell, H., *The Woodstock, Sumner, and Buckfield Town Register, 1905.* (H. E. Mitchell Company, 1905)

Goodyear, F., Bassett, E., Daggett F., Mitchell, H., *The Town Register: Standish, Baldwin, Cornish, Limerick, Limington, 1905.* (H. E. Mitchell Company, 1905)

Taylor, R., Lord, E., *History of Limington Maine.* (Heritage Books, 1991)//

Ellis, A., *The Story of Stockton Springs, Maine* (Historical Committee of Stockton Springs, 1955)

Peters, J., *Prevailing Westerlies* (Destiny Image Incorporated, 1988)

Rideout, D., The History of Pentecost in Maine, bible.exchange/books/daniel-rideout-articles-biographies/page/the-history-of-pentecost-in-maine

Priolo, G., NavSource Online: Service Ship Photo Archive, USS YP-414, http://navsource.org/archives/14/31414.htm

New England Ski History, Big Squaw Mountain, newenglandskihistory.com/Maine/squawmtn.php

"Open House Sunday At New Nursing Home," *Daily Kennebec Journal*, Volume CXLV, No. 63, pp. 19-20 (Augusta: Kennebec Journal, 1970)

Kirkpatrick, G., Influenza 1918: A Maine Perspective, digitalcommons.library.umaine.edu/mainehistoryjournal/vol25/iss3/3/

Spaeth, E., Andrews, J., Dash, G., Wyman, E., Hurd, A., Bull, F., Lepore, A., The Journal of The Maine Medical Association, archive.org/details/journalofmaineme46unse/page/n6/mode/1up?view=theater

Maines Paper and Heritage Museum, Otis Mill, Jay, 1907, mainememory.net/record/98633

Stubbs A., Burrage, H., Little, G., *Genealogical and Family History of the State of Maine.* (Lewis Historical publishing Company, 1909)